Between them, **Lesley Harris** and **Caroline Spencer** have more than forty years of experience working with and owning dogs. Caroline's early career was in nursing, and she believes the empathy necessary when caring for people is equally as important when working with d   She has two children and five dogs. Caroline is author of *Why L My Dog Do That?* and designer of the Ultimate Happy At Heel H   ss. For the last twenty years she has worked with owners on a one-to-one basis, and also gives talks on communicating effectively w   puppies and problem dogs.

For many years Lesley worked with preschool children, and found this experience to be an invaluable aid when working with puppies, as   methods used for education and guidance proved to be surprisin iy similar.

Having bred puppies in the past, Lesley and Caroline are very aware how easily well-meaning ignorance can lead to long-term issues in the adult dog. They are passionate about making prospective owners fully awa   ' the huge responsibility involved in taking a puppy into their lives   eir joint passion is in discovering a better way to communicate with dogs in order to improve the lives of pets and owners alike, whether it be following the latest scientific research in all things, from food to canine emotions, or simply observing canine behaviour in all its for.

Praise for Caroline and Lesley

'Using insight and experience, this book gives you the best start possible with your new dog.'

Brenda Aloff, Heaven On Arf Training Center, USA

'This book is brimming with practical advice on how dogs think and learn, and how to live cooperatively and harmoniously with our canine friends.'

1 Concern

Also by Caroline Spencer and available from Constable & Robinson

Why Does My Dog Do That?

Parenting Your New Puppy

Caroline Spencer and Lesley Harris

A How To Book

ROBINSON

ROBINSON

First published in Great Britain in 2016 by Robinson

A CIP catalogue record for this book
is available from the British Library.

ISBN: 978-1-47213-623-7 (paperback)
Typeset in Great Britain by TW Type, Cornwall
Printed and bound in Great Britain by Clays Ltd, St Ives plc
Papers used by Robinson are from well-managed forests and other responsible sources

MIX
Paper from
responsible sources
FSC
www.fsc.org   FSC® C104740

Robinson
is an imprint of
Little, Brown Book Group
Carmelite House
50 Victoria Embankment
London EC4Y 0DZ

An Hachette UK Company
www.hachette.co.uk

www.littlebrown.co.uk

How To Books are published by Robinson, an imprint of Little, Brown Book
Group. We welcome proposals from authors who have first-hand experience
of their subjects. Please set out the aims of your book, its target market and its
suggested contents in an email to Nikki.Read@howtobooks.co.uk

Contents

Acknowledgements

We would like to give a massive thank you to PDSA principal vet Paul Manktelow BVMS MSc MRCVS for his continuing support, and for writing our foreword. Also huge thanks and gratitude for two very eminent authors (and more) in the canine field, Catherine O'Driscoll of Canine Health Concern, and Brenda Aloff, the all-American canine behaviour trainer, who have given us their backing with their kind words and guidance. Most importantly, we thank all our dogs past and present who have given us such love and insight into their canine minds, and all the dogs and owners whom we have met and have had the privilege of working with over the years.

Sincere thanks to Clive Hebard (managing editor), and particularly to Charlotte Cole (editor), at Little, Brown, for their unbelievable patience and understanding. Writing this book – 'our baby' – was a very personal thing for both of us, so to our minds, untouchable. Both Clive and Charlotte handled our occasional 'toys out the pram' moments beautifully, and with the help of Charlotte's amazing editing we are now very proud parents!

Foreword by Paul Manktelow
BVMS MSc MRCVS

Paul Manktelow is principal vet at PDSA UK. He appears regularly on our TV screens in a number of prime-time programmes in the UK.

Raising a puppy is a huge responsibility and, if done correctly, can lead to a lifetime of happiness and friendship between you and your dog. If done badly, a lifetime of stress and misery can ensue for both parties. With an ever expanding array of websites, blogs and social media forums, it is easy to become overwhelmed by the sheer volume of advice on offer. But what advice is good advice?

The most valuable source of knowledge must surely be from someone with a wealth of experience. Hearsay and anecdotes can have no place during the delicate process of raising a puppy. This book gives sound advice for everyday situations you will face with your new canine companion, starting from the moment you first set eyes on him. The following pages are not meant as a text book or recipe to create the perfect puppy, but aim to present the principles behind a way of thinking that encourages a relationship of trust. This can then be applied to almost any situation you and your dog will encounter. A relationship where both parties respect and trust each other is destined to succeed.

We all like to think we know best, it is human nature after all. But hidden within these pages I guarantee you will find a pearl of wisdom you did not know before, whether you have a puppy with a pre-existing problem or you are a puppy parent-to-be. Sometimes, no matter how much experience you have training puppies, a fresh perspective on how they think and learn can be a real eye-opener.

Introduction

Parenting Your New Puppy is all about giving you a comprehensive understanding of the puppy you are hoping to take into your home – whether from a breeder or a rescue – and helping you to make good choices based on that knowledge.

One size does not fit all with puppies, as with children. Through our considerable experience with both, we know that the response of children and puppies to gentle guidance is remarkably similar. We want to show you how to see your puppy for what he is – an intelligent being, who deserves a much wider education than the traditional 'human control' format of sit, stay, heel and the rest. He deserves to be taught in a way that is both calm and fun, and that relates to his natural instincts. He needs an owner who will protect him from danger and stress, as a parent would a child. By following the information and guidelines in this book, and your natural instincts, you will be able to do just that.

Do Dogs and Humans have Similar Emotions?

It has taken millions of years for humans to become civilised, yet beneath that thin veneer of civilisation is a caveman or woman just needing the trigger to emerge! Any mother will feel that primitive, savage rush which comes if her child is in danger, or is simply made to feel unhappy by another person (and in that moment it is only the millennia of civilisation which stops her from attacking the culprit). Men do not need much prodding by another man for their latent caveman to emerge – witness any town centre on a Friday night!

Dogs have lived with us for thousands of years, and have progressively evolved to fit in with our human ways, but if humans need very little to strip away the constraints of civilisation, how much less will it take for our canine companions to revert – to remember how to be wild dogs?

We have to acknowledge that we are very similar in many ways to these less 'evolved' mammals, but never lose sight of the fact that dogs and humans are different. Love your dog as you would any member of your family – but respect that he is a canine. Beneath the soft furry exterior there is a wild animal tamed only because of our mutual needs and wish for coexistence. Most importantly, remember that canines neither fully understand nor embrace our compassionate human ways.

That said, it is without doubt that dogs do grieve for lost companions both human and canine. Of course, this is because their loss affects them personally in a negative way, just as for us. However, we have both observed, many times, the 'nothing in it for me' caring and nurturing which a fit and healthy dog will show for its older or less able canine companion. They will take protective action if their companion is threatened by another creature, even if there is a danger of physical harm to themselves. Of course, this could be dismissed as pack mentality kicking in, protect the pack at all costs – but we have also seen a dog lying quietly by the side of his sick friend, just to give the comfort of his presence. If you subscribe to the pack mentality idea, isn't the sick dog of no further use? So why waste time and energy giving him comfort?

Why is it that when you are feeling low your dog will often give you the comfort of joining you and touching you in a gentle and loving way, or simply 'being' with you? This does not fit into the comfortable 'dogs cannot feel love or any of the more complex emotions', school of thought. But seeing is believing, and we have both observed this, and many other apparently inexplicable behaviours.

Dogs can never be humans in fluffy coats, nor should we want them to be. But always remember that there is a lot more which brings us together than divides us. Love, loyalty, unconditional sacrifice and care for our young; anger, fear, sorrow, happiness. All of these emotions are common to both humans and dogs.

Teaching Children and Puppies

Very young children and puppies have no concept of fair, unfair, good, bad, sharing, unselfishness, sacrifice or any of the 'civilised' behaviours, except when they apply to themselves. They are totally self-orientated, and they will do whatever it takes to survive, without thought or compassion for anyone, or anything, else. They have no concept of guilt – for them threat has to equal action. Action equals a result for self.

This primal focus to survive at all costs, and in any way they can, is common to the young of all species. As they grow up, puppies do learn restraint and self-discipline, and how to fit in with both humans and canines, and this involves the ability to compromise, cooperate and become a 'team player' – but of course they never develop the progressively complex understanding of a human child.

It is up to the parents of human children to gently counter their more savage urges, to temper and direct their behaviours. They lightly guide their children towards a more socially acceptable way of behaving, and at the same time instil in them the moral code which will encourage them to develop self-control and self-discipline, and use their conscience to guide them through life.

Both children and dogs are taught and moulded – in many areas directly counter to their *natural* reactions – in order to produce well-adjusted, well-balanced and socially acceptable members of our *human* society.

With a human child we apply this approach to every area of his life until he grows up knowing right from wrong, to have compassion for others, and understands how to fit in and be a useful member of the society in which he will live.

If we did not take the trouble to curb and direct (and in some cases completely countermand) his natural instincts for the sake of a cohesive and workable society, we would end up with a feral child – one who does not understand the concept of socially acceptable behaviour. He would be outcast, condemned through no fault of his own simply because he had ignorant parents who either did not bother, or did not understand, how to nurture and direct him.

The most tragic aspect to this is that the child is deeply unhappy. He knows that somehow he does not fit in, that everything he does is wrong in the eyes of society. Not knowing how to behave in a socially acceptable way, he might go down the path of aggression and increasingly disruptive behaviour in an effort to feel some measure of control and self-worth. Or perhaps he will become painfully shy and withdrawn – unable to understand how to behave in a way that is acceptable to his peers – and feeling unable to do right for doing wrong, decides it is safer to become invisible.

This is the scenario for every socially unacceptable dog. The owner who takes the trouble to understand, to guide and direct, to establish consistent and reasonable boundaries, will never end up with a disruptive, aggressive, 'shut down' or generally unacceptably behaved dog (unless a medical problem is the underlying issue).

Dogs will *never* develop a conscience, but they will understand that we do not accept certain very natural behaviours. And because – if we do our job right – they will accept and respond to every request we make of them, they will learn to curb their instinctive responses.

Unlike children who grow into human adults with advanced and elaborate brains, dogs will probably never understand *why* we ask such unnatural behaviours of them. But because the way in which their brains react to information, situations and instructions is so much less complicated than ours, they will accept our requests without question if we provide the right answers to their simple and fundamental questions, and prove that we will always provide for them, keep them safe and make good decisions.

They ask no more than this – except for our friendship.

How Things Go Wrong

With children, a good parent understands the need for the gentle guidance which helps them through rough patches, and shows them how to cope. If the same gentle guidance and empathy is shown to puppies, they too will grow up in a well-balanced and acceptable way, but unfortunately all too often this is not their lot in life.

Puppies are often expected to be the perfect companion just because the human says so. They are given little guidance; they are punished for inappropriate behaviour, but not shown what appropriate behaviour is. Then they are blamed for their response.

In the UK, the PDSA in 2105 reported five million pet owners did no research at all before taking on their pet, with many largely unaware of the specific needs of their chosen pet. When we are called in to help owners with their dog-related problems, the cause of these problems is always the result of the misunderstanding of how to communicate. The owner is ignorant of the reasons for their puppy's behaviour, and therefore cannot educate their puppy in a way that will ensure a stress-free and mutually satisfying life together.

The owner often blames the puppy, and then becomes angry, disheartened, and ends up making the problems ten times worse. The owner loses the will to help their dog, simply because quite honestly (and understandably) they really don't like it any more.

They then either give up, and the puppy goes to a rescue centre, or they continue to battle on, making the problems worse (often resulting in a dog with lifelong issues). Or they call us in. We do what we can and achieve very good results, but a damaged dog will never be as good as a dog who was educated correctly from the start.

Our Approach to this Book

In *Parenting Your New Puppy* we have endeavoured to give you all the information needed to bring your puppy up in the best way.

We take our hats off to the people who have studied and made a lifetime commitment to uncovering the mysteries of canine behaviour, and we have most gratefully used their findings to scientifically clarify and expand our knowledge of the 'truths' we have observed through living a lifetime with dogs. But we have tried not to go too in depth in this book, as in our experience owners just want a simple method for bringing up their new puppy. Instead, we have concentrated on what we believe to be the most important points – what to consider before taking on a puppy, and what we have learned through experience to be the stumbling blocks of misunderstanding between human and canine, which can scupper the relationship before it has even begun.

When a dog reaches maturity, some behaviours require more detailed explanation, but this book is for new owners of puppies up to six months, and we believe that in these early days just the basic reasons for behaviour are enough to be going on with. With a relaxed and mutually respectful relationship established, if more complex issues arise the owner can address them from a solid foundation of trust, and the frantic fire-fighting which causes so much stress and misery for all concerned, can be avoided.

However, although this book is all about prevention rather than cure, if you are currently tearing your hair out because of your puppy's unacceptable behaviour, do not despair! You will see in Chapter 17, Preventing Common Dog Problems, that the means of re-educating your puppy are very similar to the ways of avoiding the behaviours in the first place. You will gain a lot from reading this book from the beginning.

Everything comes down to understanding why your puppy does what he does. When you have this, your attitude changes from one of anger and defensive 'What is *wrong* with you? I give you everything, and you treat me like this!' to 'Oh my goodness I never *realised*, I feel terrible!'

Our experience of working with many dog owners is that 'ideal' is very rarely the norm. If it were, then there would be very few dogs in domestic situations, and the human and canine world would be the poorer for it.

The invaluable experience of applying theory in real-life situations, where the fundamental 'rules' must still be implemented, has given us the insight to see that there is never a 'one size fits all' solution to problems. We also know that the perfect home, where *all* the boxes that would provide an ideal environment for a puppy are ticked, is rarely available. Providing a caring owner is prepared to acknowledge and work around any less-than-ideal scenarios, their puppy can still live a happy, fulfilled life.

Just think about it – it is completely unnatural for a puppy to leave its mother at ten weeks to live with another species, but given a kind and knowledgeable owner, puppies still thrive. This makes it clear just how wonderfully adaptable and suited to living with humans dogs can be. Provided they have an owner who is prepared to understand and meet their physical and emotional needs, they really can learn to fit in with our vastly differing lifestyles without stress.

In *Parenting Your New Puppy* we will guide you through the process of finding a puppy. The questions to ask the breeders or rescue centre, and what to look for in a litter. We take you from your first day at home – and those first few traumatic nights – through to taking your puppy out into the world. We teach you how to engage with age-appropriate play with your puppy, which will really teach him everything he needs to know about living in this human world. We also steer you through the ways of preventing the most common behavioural problems we see on a regular basis in our work with dogs, young and old.

We do not train children, we bring them up. We should not 'train' puppies either. We hope this book will give you an easily understood, realistic and effective way of interacting with your puppy, and set the foundations of a seamless move forward into a well-balanced, joyful life together – with room for manoeuvre, and without compromising the essentials for your puppy to live a stress-free and happy life.

Paws for Thought

For ease of reading, we refer to a puppy as 'he' throughout the book, but our advice applies to both sexes, unless otherwise stated.

Introduction by Patch and Truffle

Whey hey . . . whoo hoo . . . yep it's me, Patch. Who am I? Well I came to live with my friend Spot. He introduced the last book and thought it would be good for me to put my paw print on this one (I am closer to being a puppy, and this book is all about puppies – and quite frankly my friend Spot is getting on a bit!). I don't remember everything that happened, some is a bit of a blur, but there is much that sticks in my mind, so here goes . . .

My earliest memories are before my eyes opened, all snuggled up to my mum and brothers and sisters. Nuzzling and sucking lovely warm milk from my mother and being tumbled about when she cleaned me up and made me pee and poop. Now and again through these early days, when I was with them all, I was also picked up by a human child, so gently, and held close to them. This was a bit weird to begin with as this person didn't smell anything like my mother, but as the days went by I began to enjoy these moments more and more.

I couldn't see anything or hear anything, but felt things as they vibrated through the floor. If it was scary I just snuggled up to Mum and that made me feel safe.

My eyes opened and a few days after that I began to hear noises too. All these new sights and sounds were fuzzy at first, but slowly became clearer. It was then I began to make out faces and other things that I'd only felt before. I could see the humans when they picked me up, so carefully, and gently smoothed me with their paws in a way which felt very nice. Thank goodness they held me low and close; that made me feel safe, too.

I remember once being picked up by someone else and they held me out at arm's length, my legs dangling in mid-air, then they brought me close to their face . . . well, that was a shock. I hoped that wouldn't happen again anytime soon, talk about scary or what! I was so glad when they put me down again and I could snuggle up to Mum. I remember thinking that the next time that human comes I would run to the furthest space and look away; hopefully then they would leave me alone.

Then it all changed! My brothers and sisters and I were all tumbled into a box, we shouted and squealed for Mummy; we heard her whining and snuffling around and digging to get to us. The box wobbled and her calls became less distant until we couldn't hear her any more. It was dark and suddenly there were slamming doors and a grumble, and then we were moving. The next thing was that the box moved again, there were lights, that's all, and we wobbled as the box was lifted and then nothing . . . absolutely diddly nothing . . . the sounds disappeared into the distance . . . we all shouted and shouted but nothing, and then we huddled together as it got darker and colder.

We must have fallen asleep because we were woken by crashing and banging, breaking glass, tins and things, human voices . . . we all shouted and clambered all over each other. 'Let us out, we are here! We're HERE!!!' . . . then the sounds disappeared and there was just silence again. It started to get really wet – water just fell from the sky. Our box melted and then, there we were, cold, wet, very hungry and no Mummy. We cried and cried, called and called . . .

After what seemed like forever – it probably wasn't as long as it felt – we heard a shout and then we heard human footsteps running in the wet puddles. It was a child human, and he bent down and picked me up. He held me close to his warm body, his lovely warm dry body, and I felt so safe as he wrapped me in his clothes. More humans arrived and we heard lots of gentle voices as we were all picked up. I looked over to one of my sisters, she wasn't moving, all I could see was her trying to say something to me, she opened her mouth but nothing happened.

I can't remember anything after that until I woke up in a snuggly warm box surrounded by all but one of my brothers and sisters. I wonder what happened. I never did see her again.

We could hear sounds of dogs all around. I wondered if Mummy was here. We called out for her, but she didn't call back. A lovely human with a quiet gentle voice came instead, and fed us lovely warm yummy milk. It didn't taste much like Mum's, but I was so hungry I didn't care.

And so that's what happened: we got fed, we got cuddles and we had each other. This place, where the humans had brought us, actually smelt more dog than human, and we heard all the crashing and banging and barking and howling and stuff, the usual noisy doggy noises, but here we also heard dogs calling to go home, dogs just wanting a home and somewhere to call their own. They had meals and were warm but more than anything they wanted their very own human; they wanted this so much that the air was filled with the smell and feel of their sadness and this desperate need . . . sorry went off track there! *Sniff sniff.*

So as I was going to say, it wasn't long after we got there, maybe a couple of days, that a grown-up dog was brought into us by one of the humans . . . oh she was so like Mummy, kind and gentle, and she bent her head as we all rushed to see her, and she *wanted* us to go to her . . . she lay down and it was then that we saw also for the first time little Truffle.

Truffle was shy but we snuggled up to her as we did each other, and we all suckled up with our new mummy dog who we all called Auntie Star . . . for the first time since we had been taken from our real mummy, we felt really safe. We had an adult we could turn to, like we did Mum, when we were a little scared or just tired.

Having Auntie Star with us was as near to a mum as you could get. She loved us and fed us and told us off if we got it wrong like any mum would. We felt safe and learned how far we could push, or not. We learned how to get along with each other and fit in. She didn't put up with bullies or with any of us pushing the others away and demanding attention all the time! We were all equals in her eyes.

So, for us, the next few weeks we spent with Auntie Star were happy times in every way. I was safe with my brothers and sisters, and the humans too. We played, and learned how to be friends with them, by not being too rough or biting too hard. Strangers came to see us – I know now they were choosing one of us to be their new friend and take us away from all we had grown to know and understand. Some of them loomed over us and picked us up high and put their faces right up to ours! Not pleasant, but I endured it because my human at the time soon put them right and asked them to hold me close and gently massage me. No one could ever do this with Truffle though; she'd wriggle constantly, and nip if need be, to get free.

Truffle sat on my head on many occasions, but as long as she didn't break wind I was happy . . . to have the closeness was so snuggly and reassuring. Us against the world! I hoped she'd come with me when I went to my new home.

My sister Truffle was a right little monkey (I know she isn't my real sister, but I feel like she is). She rushed up to people left, right and centre. Nibbled and jumped in their faces. When she did that to her mum or us we would walk away, she wasn't a lot of fun to be around. She said, where she'd come from, the humans used to swing her round and do a lot of shouting (they shall not be named for confidentiality reasons) – she was held up high and rough and tumbled. She just never learned that the human touch can be a gentle experience, and so never learned to be gentle in return. She wasn't smoothed and held gently at all, and so didn't like to be held a lot and wriggled free if she could, and mouthed a lot, which either got her put down or shouted at! I felt sorry for her as it was not her fault. If only she had been held like I had been held, I'm sure she would have been less stressed and far more accepting. Those first couple of weeks must have been awful. She wasn't good at trusting people – no surprise there really.

Then all change again! That was when the humans found me a new home with Uncle Spot. I do love him. I'm not sure he was too thrilled when I first pitched up, me launching in with 'play with me' and stuff. I know when he wants his nap now, and quite honestly I nap right there with him. Perfectly lovely. He puts me in my place when I get too annoying.

I suddenly had to grow up. With the help of my humans and of course Uncle S. I was helped to accept and not be worried about stuff, as they always showed me what they wanted if I looked confused. I wasn't pressured to be a performing robot. We had fun and I learned through play at home, had friends round to play, went round to theirs and learned to relax and chill with or without my owners, and with and without Uncle S. I was allowed to be me.

They seemed to understand what made me happy, and what made me scared, and always made me feel that they knew the best things to do when I wasn't sure. They made me feel safe, and that I fitted in.

Life was good and soon I didn't miss Auntie Star so much and enjoyed my life as a dog with my humans and Uncle Spot. I felt safe knowing they were there for me. They chose my friends wisely and never put me in awkward situations for me to 'get used to it'. They are always there to guide and protect me. I trust them and love them with all my heart and paws. I'm one lucky fella. I am understood, and that makes me very happy.

When Truffle came to live with us a month or so ago, it turned out that she had had a completely different upbringing to mine. She was expected to learn sit, stay, heel and 'don't play' in a room which was noisy and full of other dogs. It was very hard to concentrate when she was with all these dogs and just wanted to play. Even when her owner had food in his hand, it wasn't food she wanted, it was to play. Sometimes when Fred the bully pup came, she'd hide under a chair, because no one stopped him being unkind to her.

The fun part of the class was when everyone gave her food, and then when they came round to her house she got food again, but when they were on a walk, suddenly it wasn't the right thing to do to go up to people and jump on them for food. She couldn't understand why it was right sometimes, but not right other times. So, to say the least, she was confused and muddled.

You remember she was forced right into people's faces? Now she had to get used to situations that frightened her, with no support from her humans, just stuck there on a lead while the other humans were allowed to put their hands all over her. Children were allowed to play roughly with her, even when she tried to show them in every way she could that she was tired or that they were hurting her. Even when she showed them that she didn't like it. Her humans did not protect her, they did not do anything to make her trust them, so the upshot was that she took matters into her own paws.

She used to run away to go and find her own fun, and also got into the habit of hiding under tables to just have her own space away from the children. She got to the stage that, when she had had enough of people saying they wanted a cuddle and not taken no for an answer, she bit them. Fair play to her, but it was her that got into trouble, not the human who had made it happen.

She kept being returned to the place where the humans who saved us lived, but every time she was taken by new humans the same things happened, so each time she was taken back again.

Things went from bad to worse until at last she found someone who understood her needs and questions and fears and concerns. That person was my human. Lucky for her, it seems, because Uncle Spot (who knows about these things) told me that another bite and it would have been her head on the chopping block! I'm not exactly sure what that means – but it does not sound good.

So now, after all our adventures, here we are, me, Uncle S., my sister Truffle and our lovely humans. One big happy family, and life is so GOOOOD!!!

CHAPTER 1

See the World from a Puppy's Point of View

Your puppy at ten to twelve weeks old is roughly the equivalent of a young toddler.

You have taken him from the only home he has ever known, from his mother and siblings, and placed him somewhere strange, with strange humans who can't speak his language, and often without another of his species in sight.

How would a toddler feel? In fact, how would *you* feel?

Paws for Thought

For both children and dogs, memories relate to self. What hurt me? What made me happy? What did I do to bring about that result?

In this chapter we share more about our approach to living with and educating puppies, before going into the practicalities of finding a puppy who is right for you in Chapter 4. Owning a dog is a big responsibility – we should apply the same rules to researching, learning and preparing to bring a puppy into our home as we would for any major life decision. For us, it is important to be able to see the world from a puppy's point of view, to know what they are experiencing. And a useful way to do this is to think about your own children when they were toddlers, or your own memories from being very young.

Children up to two years old and puppies of up to sixteen weeks have been scientifically proven to display very similar basic emotions. They also use similar body language to convey important messages. Neither are naughty or aggressive. But both can be confused or upset. Both need understanding and guidance. Neither have command of verbal language. We must understand their needs by learning how they use body language in their efforts to communicate. If you watch you will learn. *They* watch and learn from you!

We are not advocating treating your puppy exactly as you would a human child, but it is very helpful to see and understand the similarities, as well as appreciate the differences – using what you do know to help you to understand the things you don't.

When raising a human child, it is best to take the time and trouble to gently guide and show – by example – how we wish him to behave. By doing this we create the kind of calm, secure, fear-free atmosphere which is conducive to learning. When he does not understand what we require of him and is only doing the wrong thing out of fear and confusion, we wouldn't punish him, but instead kindly and calmly show him how to get it right.

For example, if your toddler is, say, chewing the remote control or twiddling the knob of the hi-fi, what would you do?

Well, in this enlightened age it is unlikely that we would roar at him, smack him and 'put the fear of God' into him. Why? Firstly, he is too young to fully understand that what he is doing is not acceptable and possibly dangerous. Secondly, it is also setting the scene for fear and misunderstanding. It is not teaching in a way that will make him trust us, to come to us with problems and in all ways to bond with us. Finally, and most importantly, he is not learning how to get things right – only the consequence of getting things wrong.

Instead, when a toddler is too young to understand right from wrong, we would use redirection. We would gently remove him from the area of conflict, and engage him in a more interesting and appropriate activity.

When he is older we would gently explain why a certain action is unacceptable, and then show him with speech and by example the acceptable way of behaving. If he understands, but deliberately defies us, we would use effective but non-violent 'consequences of action'.

You can use exactly the same principle with puppies. Of course, your puppy will never understand *why*, but he will learn what is acceptable behaviour if taught by example in a non-verbal, canine-appropriate way.

All young creatures need to learn boundaries and self-control, and all need the feeling of security and trust engendered by a calm and gentle parent-figure who gives them choices to help them learn. The way we tap into the psyche of a human child may be different to a canine, but their fundamental needs are surprisingly similar.

Of course your puppy has to learn how to fit in with *your* life, to behave in a socially acceptable way so far as human society is concerned (which will often not reflect natural canine responses – so you will be persuading him against his instincts in many cases), but how you go about this will make all the difference to your future relationship with your dog. Rather than thinking of yourself as a 'boss', think of yourself as a surrogate parent to your puppy – because this is what he needs.

If you take the time to read books by informed people who have been studying canine behaviour for decades (we list a few in the Resources Section), observe the way dogs interact with each other, how their body language changes when confronted with different situations, and then *comprehend* that canine language, it becomes very easy to be kind and understanding, to gently show your dog what you require of him, without being confusing.

For Lesley, engaging with her adored grandchildren in the past few years has reinforced hugely her belief in the common characteristics of children and puppies, and how similar are the strategies required to show them how to develop as good citizens. Her daughter is taking a degree in childcare. Reading the guidelines for early years care, Lesley has found it extremely interesting to note that, from birth to eighteen months, you could easily substitute the word 'puppy' for 'baby' in almost all situations. The psychology behind the care, and the methods for achieving results, are pretty much identical.

Through scientific study it has become apparent that many drives and core behaviours are extremely similar across many species – and dogs are top of the list when comparing some of the more unusual similarities between human and other mammals. In fact, interestingly, only two animals have the 'left-sided gaze'. One is the human – when facing a person, we unconsciously look to the left when trying to work out their emotional state. The only other animal to do this is our friend the dog! Similarly, only humans, dolphins and dogs can follow the direction of a pointed finger with ease.

Living in a dog pack, in a non-human 'wild' environment, a puppy will stay with his mother, siblings and other pack members for many months or more, usually upwards of two years. During this time he will learn everything he needs to know about canine etiquette – the importance of cooperation, how to give and take, when to stand firm and when to yield, and how to react and behave when presented with every possible scenario which living as a dog presents – in short, how to survive and prosper harmoniously within his family and wider environment. All this he will learn gradually and naturally from his mother, siblings and other pack members.

At eight and a half weeks he has only just begun to understand his place in the world, and is beginning to have the confidence to move away to investigate on his own. Yet humans decree that this is the best time to uproot him. We prefer puppies to stay with their mum until they are ten or twelve weeks, as the social fear period is between eight and ten weeks. His mother will steer him through this, but, without her help, new situations that frighten him could have long term negative effects. For this reason, we believe that a puppy benefits greatly from this longer period of wise maternal guidance.

Take into account his immaturity and consider yourself to be a surrogate parent; using all the understanding and knowledge you will gain from reading this book, you will be well on your way to having the stress free, relaxed and happy companion.

Puppies and children need to learn socially acceptable behaviour; they need to learn boundaries and *self*-discipline; they also need to know that, at times, they must instantly follow a command (not a request – which is what you should be issuing for most of the time), just because you say so, for safety reasons.

This will happen naturally if you take the time and trouble to earn your puppy's respect and trust, and not 'sergeant-major' him into submission.

The first will give you a friend for life, and a dog who will do as you ask in any situation because he trusts you and respects your judgement implicitly – the second, a robot who performs like a trick pony, and has not one ounce of understanding *of* you, or connection *to* you.

Paws for Thought

Puppies and babies don't have a hidden agenda. They just want to please and be understood. Don't crush their self-esteem by shouting negatives at them for being themselves, and for trying to communicate with you their way. Don't shut pups away in a cage for your convenience unless it is for a short time for their safety – these experiences will stay with them for a lifetime. With puppies, the social fear period kicks in at eight to ten weeks prior to this they will exuberantly discover everything with no fear. They will get many things wrong, but put them right in a thinking manner. The more appropriate attention they receive, the better they will respond and bond with you.

The Formative Weeks

In the last two years we have asked each and every client where they got their dog. If it was a puppy, we asked at what age they picked him up, and where he was housed in the first few weeks of life with his mother. Time and time again we heard that the puppy was picked up by the new owner before eight weeks of age. More commonly than we'd like, we also heard that they were housed in a shed or kennel away from normal home living conditions, resulting in very little human interaction in their formative weeks.

Where we have been asked by clients to check a litter before they choose a puppy, we are often alarmed to find that the mother has been taken away from the puppies just after weaning, at four to five weeks of age. The reason the breeders give is that the puppies have sharp teeth and claws, or they bug her too much. But she is their mother and she can manage her puppies! Yes, breast feeding can be uncomfortable at times (ask any mother) but a good breeder will carefully file sharp 'baby' claws to minimise the scratching of the mother's belly. And as for teeth? Well canine mothers have been dealing with sharp puppy teeth since the dawn of time – they can cope! If the pups are in a space where the mother can leap in and out, then she is quite capable of giving herself a break when she chooses.

Puppies need their mother's milk and their mother – in our eyes there is no alternative. The vital antibodies from their mother to protect them from disease are paramount to health and wellbeing, and the security and bonding that unrestricted access to her puppies will give is beyond price to both mother and offspring. So the longer the time they have with their mother, the healthier and happier the puppy will be and, ultimately, the better chance he will have of becoming a healthy, happy, well-balanced adult.

We have rarely come across a dog with massive issues about fitting into to a family home environment, fearful of even his own shadow, when he was first homed at ten to twelve weeks of age, from a family environment in a loving stable home with the buzz of gentle children and family.

Paws for Thought

All you have to do (on many occasions) is stand back and watch how 'well-balanced' dogs interact with each other. You will learn how to approach everything you do with them in a far more natural way, and how to form the connection you desire.

Educating with Life Skills

Training, traditionally, has had as its prime focus teaching the dog to respond to certain commands at any given time – either to stop an unacceptable behaviour, or to control the dog to be obedient to commands such as sit, stay and heel – and of course 'come back'. We believe that this kind of obedience training is restrictive, as the dog responds without thought or understanding. In addition, any puppy, no matter how naturally confident and strong-minded, is too young for this kind of rigid training and it can create huge stress, leading to complex problems in many puppies as they grow to adulthood.

Just imagine teaching all this to a child? Would it work? Would they be really relaxed in your company? If you take the time and trouble to create a bond of trust and mutual respect with your dog, he will choose to follow your lead and respond to your requests. Walking with you, recall to you, will occur naturally without bribery or force, and can be reinforced without dominance. Your dog will fit into your lifestyle because he is allowed to think for himself and chose (with guidance) the best way to live in harmony with his human. Other desirable behaviours will follow without the need to 'train' him to obey.

Paws for Thought

The Problem with Sit

There is a school of thought that states: if you get a dog to sit, there are many, many things it can't do – get into trouble being highest on that list. In our opinion, the only very important thing it won't be able to do is to think for itself.

Do we tell our children randomly to 'Sit!' in every situation? We may say, 'OK sit down for a moment and speak with me', in order to calm them down, but not as a panacea for all ills.

If a pup can't do it, he is not getting it wrong – we are teaching him badly. We are teaching him something that no other dog has ever asked of another, and the pupil is just asking, 'Why?' and 'What's the point?' What's more, getting a puppy to sit and stay is not physically good for him. Research has shown it is detrimental to good physical health in the young, putting too much pressure on young spines and joints, let alone their immature cognitive ability. If we are teaching him the sit in order to stop another behaviour, then we are crushing the pup's natural language, and frustration will set in and behavioural issues (such as nipping and tail chasing) begin through undue stress.

For example, many are advised to get a puppy or young dog to sit in a shop doorway and watch the world go by. Cars and bikes and strange dogs go past. Humans will go past, making eye contact. When allowed to behave naturally, if a dog is worried by a situation it would get out of there and reassess from a safe distance – and this is exactly what you should be doing for him as he is restricted by a lead and unable to follow his natural instincts. Instead, these dogs are told to 'sit there and be quiet'. Your puppy needs choices, and you will have to help him with these because he will generally be attached to you by a lead. You need to have buckets of empathy when you take him out and about.

Bribery doesn't work, either; what it does is get the child or dog to only perform when you have food or gifts. If you buy a child everything he wants, when he wants it, then all you are to that child is a money bank or a present giver. If the child or puppy gets attention for doing the wrong thing, then that turns it into a way to get your attention. They've trained you to stop whatever you are doing and look at them. We're not in any way asking you to ignore bad behaviour, but we will show you how to deal with it in a silent and proactive manner.

Exercises such as 'come back' and walking with you are necessary in our world, primarily for safety, but they happen naturally anyway where dogs are left to their own devices. For instance, village dogs in Turkey and Cyprus have no human home, but live together, within a human environment, in mutually beneficial packs. They do not 'train' the other dogs in their pack, nor their puppies, but bring them up in a way they understand, as we do with our children, teaching them life skills. Their rules are simple, and as they bring up their young, they also educate them in an effortlessly natural way. The family sticks together, looks out for each other, feeds together, plays together and, all importantly, rests and relaxes together. How to just be themselves in a socially acceptable manner is the greatest gift of education you can give any child or any dog.

Dogs and children are born with no behavioural issues; it is what happens in their lives which moulds them into what they become. It's what you do, from day one, which will cause the puppy or child to turn into a well-balanced adult dog or human – or not.

Do not expect your puppy to be exactly the same as his parents or siblings – or your last dog of the same breed for that matter. All have differing personalities and behaviours, some of which are enhanced by selective breeding – guarding, or rounding up by nipping heels, hunting or retrieving, but they all live by the same rules – and understand these inbuilt canine rules absolutely. It is for *us* to understand the rules by which your individual dog would naturally live, and to work with, rather than against, them.

Some say you have to get it right by twelve months old or you have lost the moment, but there is no standard timescale for your dog to learn. Just like humans, each dog has its own personality and ability to learn – some slowly, others catch on like lightning – it is up to you to understand your puppy and go at *his* pace – not the pace at which you feel he should be progressing.

Don't force your puppy to be an adult before he's been a puppy. Don't force him to conform to our human adult expectations and stress him out. All you want for both children and puppies is for them to grow up and feel safe with you. And both will do all you ask if you educate with compassion and understanding, with less pressure to get it right from the word go.

Your primary focus should be in showing him how to fit in and thrive in your world, and for this you need patience and understanding . . . the rest actually comes naturally. Just like with children, your puppy will become an adult, and a wonderful one at that, if you give him guidance, understanding and love in equal portions.

Paws for Thought

Respect the completely different species that is canine, understand that dogs can never be human (nor should we want them to be), but use what we have in common as a base, and then read and learn from thosen who have spent a lifetime observing dogs. Study dogs and observe their behaviours yourself, then use that knowledge to better understand both the similarities *and* the differences of our two species.

CHAPTER 2

Ask Not What Your Puppy Can Do For You

Each person has their own reasons for taking a puppy into their life, so it is important to decide from the start – before you choose your puppy – exactly what you require from him. We will then look at what *he* will require from *you*.

Most people say they would like a calm, friendly, responsive and well-mannered companion, but how else do you see your puppy's future role in your life?

Some people want their dog with them at all times, and that means sitting on their lap when they are relaxing, in their car, at their place of work, on their bed – in fact the dog will be their constant companion, rarely spending time away from them. In some cases their dog might take the place of a child, husband or wife. And that is all fine, as long as you remember he is a *dog*. His presence on your sofa or bed is by your invitation only, curtailed when you decide, and that he never has the right to demand. Clearly defined roles are what give him peace of mind, security – he knows the rules and knows that they do not vary – and provide a stress-free existence for a dog.

Other people want their dog to *be* a dog and to them this means that he does not accompany them to bed, does not sit on them and does not go to work with them (and, of course, a suitable plan will be in place for him if this should be the case). They will play with him and give him affection, but will never become 'soppy' or imagine he has human emotions – in fact he must never cross the line between being a dog and a surrogate human. This is often the case when a dog has been taken for a specific purpose – to do a job of work – and dogs will be fine with this less emotional view of them, just so long as their human is also kind and just.

Many people want a dog to join their family with children, with the twin reasons that firstly it is good for their kids to have the character-building experience of caring for a vulnerable creature – it is a valuable life lesson in teaching them compassion and responsibility – and secondly, of course, it is a chance for that very special, uniquely enriching and never forgotten bond that can exist between a child and a dog to be forged.

Some people will think, 'Blimey, that's a bit deep – I just wanted a dog!', but for most people, if they really think about it, there *will* usually be more to it than that. The majority of people fall somewhere in between these categories and all of these scenarios will be just fine for your chosen companion. And whatever your reason for having a dog, the basic ground rules are the same.

Your Suitability

So, you have decided that you and your family will benefit from the enriching presence of a puppy. It will – good choice!

But how suitable are you for a puppy? It is important to consider every angle, for instance:

◆ What will be your puppy's daily routine? Do you have time to walk, play with and educate him?

◆ Will someone be with him for the majority of the day? If you do work full time, have you thoroughly researched suitable dog walkers or daycare?

◆ Have you owned a dog before, and if so was the relationship easy and rewarding for both of you? In other words, was your dog a source of pride and enjoyment for you – or embarrassment and stress?

◆ Do you have a suitable home in which to easily accommodate a dog? Does it have a garden or other enclosed outdoor space?

◆ Have you considered the impact on your previously spotlessly clean home – and your landscaped and perfect garden?

◆ If you have children, do they understand the responsibility involved when caring for a vulnerable creature?

◆ Have you researched a secure and knowledgeable place at which your dog can stay if you go away without him?

◆ And last but not least, can you afford the upkeep?

Let's think about all of these questions in more detail.

Will someone be with him for the majority of the day?

Dogs are naturally pack animals – in other words, family animals. They have evolved to become man's companion. They *crave* company. A lonely dog is an unhappy dog – and will develop all kinds of stressed behaviours which can more often than not lead to it becoming a problem dog. Do you have time to walk, play with and educate him? If you will be away from your dog for a whole working day (which, if commuting, can be ten or eleven hours of solitary confinement for a dog), and you cannot arrange for a friend or relative to be his companion for at least two thirds of that time, you must make provision – which either means a recommended dog walker or 'doggy daycare'. Ask yourself this very important question: Why are you getting a dog at a stage in your life when you cannot be the companion he needs?

Have you owned a dog before, and if so was the relationship easy and rewarding for both of you?

If you've lived with the 'perfect' dog who gave you no problems at all, you must have been doing a lot that was right. But bear in mind, dogs are *so* adaptable and willing to fit in that very often it is not until you come across a problem that you realise just how little you know about how their minds work. We often hear, 'I've had this breed all my life and have *never* had a problem until now!' With the correct training, your dog can be changed from being a source of emparrassment and stress to one of pride and enjoyment.

Do you have a suitable home in which to easily accommodate a dog?

If you do not have a garden, or at least some kind of enclosed area directly accessed from your door, the logistics of your puppy's toilet training, and later on his ability to simply go out and relieve himself, could be prohibitive – particularly if you live a few floors up in a block of flats.

Of course, all new owners will need to endure the freezing (and often wet) period of accompanying their new puppy into the garden each time he wakes, feeds or simply looks as if he needs to relieve himself – but this period is finite, and ends when the puppy gets the idea of asking to go out, going out on his own and relieving himself without the need for company. Just when the initial enthusiasm, the 'I don't mind – bless him' is wearing off, your puppy is learning to 'go solo'!

But if you do not have a secure enclosed area for him to do his business in, the 'accompanied pooping and peeing' never ends. Firstly, you will have to use a harness and lead from the word go – not desirable when it is far better to introduce this piece of equipment gradually and progressively. Secondly, even if your dog has a strong bladder, he will still need to relieve himself when necessary, and the process of donning outdoor clothes and removing yourself from a nice warm room into a windy, rainy, freezing night, will soon lose any of the appeal that it had in the first place – and what if your poor pooch has an upset tummy and rouses you at 3 a.m. with a desperate need to relieve himself?

The alternative is to continue to use newspapers and puppy pads.

This is totally unnatural for a dog once he is out of the 'nappy' stage. When he has become an adult, a dog would never mess in the den area, and this would be a source of stress to him (if he becomes very unsettled you could find that your whole flat has turned into one giant canine toilet – the puppy pads, litter tray or whatever you have provided for his needs, totally ignored). Quite frankly, it is not a viable alternative.

Of course many dogs *do* live very happily in apartments. Their owners have worked through the difficulties and have accepted the problems and extra work that having no outside access brings – they consider it a small price to pay for the joy of living with their dog. However, these problems are very real, and they *do* have to be carefully assessed and viewed, without rose-coloured spectacles. If you live in a flat or apartment with no outdoor access, make sure that you are prepared to go the extra mile to make the effort required.

Have you considered the impact on your previously spotlessly clean home – and your landscaped and perfect garden?

Even if you have cleverly picked a small, short-haired, non-shedding breed, your house and garden will probably never be the same again! That is not to say that you will be condemned to living in a smelly, chewed, dug-up, dwelling (if you follow the advice in this book, you should be able to direct your puppy's behaviour along less-traumatic lines), but with the best will in the world, as any parent will tell you, neither children nor puppies equal 'show home'.

If you have children, do they understand the responsibility involved when caring for a vulnerable creature?

Young children love pets. Young children also love cuddly toys, but will treat them rather less than gently on occasion for no discernible reason (to an adult mind). And children often view puppies and cuddly toys in the same light.

The relationship between a child and dog can be magical – but it can also be a source of fear and misery for the dog, and extreme danger to the child. Before you get a puppy, make absolutely sure that your children understand that a dog has needs and feelings, just as they do. Ask them to read Patch and Truffle's introduction to this book (pages xvi-xxvi). Find a friend with a friendly older dog and teach them to greet him appropriately. Pass on the knowledge you have gained from this book, in an age-appropriate way. Take them to your local rescue centre, where there will often be talks on puppies and other help available. In every way, make them aware and respectful of what it takes to give their puppy a happy life.

When you bring the puppy home, restrict your children's access to times when you can supervise. If you have very young children (toddlers or babies), make sure they are supervised at all times. You cannot leave children too young to understand how to treat animals alone with a dog, even for a few seconds – it is unfair on both child and dog, and very, very dangerous.

If you consider this advice unnecessary or find all this too much effort – please, do not get a dog.

Have you researched a secure and knowledgeable place at which your dog can stay if you go away without him?

Do you have obliging parents or friends who would be happy to look after your dog when you go on holiday? Alternatively, dog walkers and doggy daycare centres often will also board the dogs they care for. If neither of these options are open to you, you will need to thoroughly research reputable kennels or professional dog sitters in your area. Personal recommendation is the best way – anyone can say anything in an advertising blurb. It is surprising how many people book their wonderful holiday, then at the last minute say, 'Oh good grief – what about the dog?' Unbelievably, this is one of the reasons that dogs are dumped in rescue centres.

Can you afford the upkeep?

Chapter 6 discusses the essentials in full, but costs will include: meals and treats, dog beds, toys, vet visits, dog walkers or doggy daycare, and holiday costs, and not forgetting there may be the need to replace chewed human belongings.

Paws for Thought

Your dog should be your companion, a valued member of your family. If you are not prepared to go to all the trouble above for this sensate, vulnerable creature – do not get a dog! Rather, wait until your life is conducive to having one.

With luck your dog will be with you for ten to fifteen years. The decision to bring a dog into your home should not be taken lightly – all too often it is, and this is one of the reasons that the rescue centres are full to bursting with unhappy, unwanted dogs. Make sure this doesn't happen to you.

Very few people set out to be cruel, but very many people are guilty of unthinking neglect. They would be horrified to realise that they fall into the category of ignorant dog owners, but are too complacent or lazy to take the trouble to learn what their dog needs and what makes their dog tick, and do not provide a stress-free home.

By reading this book, you are taking the right first step. If you have read this chapter and thought, yes, I still want a dog, then read on. We will guide you through the process of choosing the right puppy, bringing him home and introducing him to the world (and how he should behave in it). The last chapter is a trouble-shooting section that we hope covers every problem your dog might start to display in his first year – and beyond!

CHAPTER 3

Double Trouble

One Puppy or Two?

Many people would like to bring home two puppies at the same time.

The advice you will hear is: do not get puppies from the same litter, they will bond together and you won't have a look-in. However, the same can be said for getting puppies from different litters.

Yes, it is great to have two dogs – canines love company, whether human or dog. But you have to have time to be with each of them individually and do lessons separately. They need to know they are both equally important to you as individuals. You also have to be prepared for double trouble.

With any dogs (or children, for that matter) there are firm boundaries to be set, and you are the one who must ultimately make all the important decisions. You must not put up with bullying – one squeezing in and pushing the other out when it comes to cuddles, or massage, or ball play, or vying for front place on the lead. They are going to have different personalities, and when they are reaching maturity things can go drastically wrong if you do not set consistent boundaries when they are puppies.

We have met families who have taken two young pups in, and either didn't notice or brushed off the signals that one was taking all the fun away from the other. In these cases, one puppy will have been pushed to take the back seat, and issues of possession aggression (with space or items) and food aggression sneak in.

If you are very experienced, and you set firm boundaries, spend time with them individually and are the one they defer to, rather than each other, you will be just fine. If you do, you are less likely to have major problems as they reach maturity if you get one of each sex.

Do not get two at the same time and expect them to rub along and keep each other entertained. You will become the B&B, the provider of a roof over their heads, and be dragged down the road to let them have their own fun in the park. They won't need your support when things get confusing or worrying – they will look to each other for that. Before you know it you have two dogs running riot, with no respect for you, no connection and zero recall. We have had too many calls and consultations about this issue.

Paws for Thought

Our advice is to have two dogs if space, time and finances allow, but with a gap between them of at least two to three years. When your first puppy has reached maturity and behaves beautifully, you are pretty safe in getting another in to join him. By doing it this way you are going to have another teacher in your midst . . . your first dog. Whether your first dog is an angel or a devil, the pup will learn by copying that behaviour.

Dogs learn by watching – always. Don't fall into the trap of thinking your dog only learns when you are specifically teaching it. As with children, they constantly learn by copying the things you do and the way you behave. You are always teaching even when you don't think you are.

In the early stages, be the one they look to because of what you do, not what you say. The clarity of your body language and signals will ensure that lessons are learned without confusion. Dogs 'misbehave' because things are unclear. They get it wrong because you have given them the wrong signals. Never blame the pupil.

We have written some guidelines in Chapter 13 to help you on your way with two puppies the same age or two dogs of different ages. But unless you have successfully raised dogs already, we strongly recommend that you get one puppy, work with him until he looks to you for all decisions and is well on the way to being a calm, well-balanced member of your family, and then look for another.

Paws for Thought

Double the trouble only if you have the expertise, time and commitment to treat them as individuals.

Adding a New Puppy to your Existing Pack

If you already have one or more dogs, the first thing to consider about adding a new puppy is the age of your existing dog or dogs. We recommend that you don't add a puppy if your dog is too young or very old.

If your existing dog is less than two years old, he is still learning his boundaries and self-discipline. A new puppy will copy both good and bad behaviours, and both dogs may well choose to bond together instead looking to you for decisions – very much like children.

If you leave it until your existing dog is in his final years, a new puppy will just be too much for the old chap.

But if you have a young dog, which you feel seems to be yearning for a canine companion, and you are confident that he is well-balanced, and not suffering from separation anxiety (see Chapter 17, pages 127–9), and your home, finances and lifestyle allow, by all means get another.

Personally, both of us always have two or more dogs, as we feel that it is great for them to have canine companionship – especially on the occasions when they are left alone. They also play canine games, which only dogs can play properly, and can reach a level of friendship and mutual care that is very heart-warming to see. That is our choice – and we are lucky enough to be able to indulge it – but a 'single' dog, given the right level of human interaction and care, can have every bit as good a life.

It is essential that, however many dogs you have, you ensure that they are all treated as individuals. Spend time with each dog on his own (even if you are all in the same space). As we have said, if you don't they will bond together, look to each other for decisions and cut you out of the picture altogether.

It is fine – wonderful, in fact – that they enjoy each other's company, but it is you to whom each and every one should look for important decisions, and you can only do this if you have worked with each on an individual basis, and have established with each one that you are the ultimate decision maker. We go into this thorny issue in more depth in Chapter 13.

If you have parented your first dog well, he will already be looking to you, and the new puppy will see this and naturally start to do the same. In other words, your job with a second puppy will be made easier, not harder, by the presence of an existing well-balanced, well-mannered dog. Your new puppy is a blank canvas, if you have taken him from a loving, knowledgeable home environment and he has no ingrained issues, and being a puppy he will naturally defer to your older dog. He will learn from him, and respect his position as an adult and an existing pack member.

The puppy is not a threat to your existing dog. You must be very careful to show him that you will take care of both him and his new companion equally. Make sure that you allow your existing dog to act like a dog, and have empathy for him in readjusting. Older dogs will put a puppy in its place if it becomes uppity – and that is a very good thing for both of them. The puppy learns canine manners and etiquette, and the older dog feels secure in his ability to keep his place in the scheme of things. There is more information about introducing a new puppy to an existing dog in Chapter 10.

If you have done your work diligently, your existing dog already thinks that you are incapable of making a poor decision and they should both settle down to enjoy a long and harmonious companionship.

If You Have an Older Dog

Some people suddenly realise that their beloved old friend is reaching the end of the road, and come to the conclusion that, 'It would be nice for Drifter to have a doggy companion.'

Trust us – it *would not* be nice for Drifter.

Drifter has lived quite happily for the past ten years or so as an 'only' dog, so why on earth, in the sunset of his years when all he wants is a warm home and a quiet life, would he want the equivalent of a baseball-cap-wearing hoodie to invade his peace and quiet?

If these people were a little more honest, the truth is more likely to be that they hope a new dog will ease the heartache when Drifter finally shuffles off his mortal coil. Or perhaps Drifter has become slow and boring, and they want to experience with a new puppy the fun they once had with Drifter when he was a young dog?

Either one is perhaps understandable – but rather less than admirable.

The bottom line is that an old dog, probably suffering from the restricted abilities and range of movement which sadly often come with old age, will almost certainly find a young boisterous puppy too much to handle (this goes for us – Lesley certainly can't skip around like she did when she was twenty, and, much as she adores her grandchildren, she tends to collapse in a heap, totally exhausted, and heave a sigh of relief when they go home!). So unless you are prepared to really go the extra mile to protect and nurture old Drifter, and to monitor and supervise the interaction between the two dogs, think more than twice about going down this road.

Drifter has given you the best years of his life; he has given you his trust, loyalty and love. The very least you can do is to repay him by caring for him in his old age, making allowances for his reduced abilities and, in every way you can, make his sunset years peaceful, secure and trouble-free.

When he dies, grieve, be grateful for all the happy years – and perhaps only *then* consider getting a new dog.

CHAPTER 4
Finding your Puppy

There are many important issues to consider before sailing forth to choose a puppy. As a family, discuss what size and type of dog is most suitable for your lifestyle. Take into consideration the size of your house, and if you have the time and energy for lively dog. Think about the size of the dog. If you have children, a very small fragile dog will need a great deal of protection from you long after he has ceased to be a puppy, as children can be less than gentle in their actions. Take the time to thoroughly discuss both what you all want, and what is practical for your particular circumstances.

Decide whether you would like a puppy from a rescue centre or from a breeder. Do you want a mixed breed, or is there a specific breed you'd prefer?

It is vitally important you consider personality as well as breed – each dog will contain different degrees of a large range of characteristics. Also research breed-specific physical problems which *can* be present (but with ethical and dedicated breeders are less likely to be). The most beautiful dog in the world can soon lose its appeal if it comes saddled with breed-related health problems (as well as deep-seated emotional issues caused by an inappropriate early environment or conditioning). With knowledgeable human owners, most emotional issues can be eradicated or at least managed to an acceptable level, but some genetic physical problems, very sadly, can be impossible to resolve.

If you want a rescue dog, look at the local and regional centres, both large and small. Research their performance and policies, visit and decide for yourself if they have the right attitude. Make sure you ask

25

all the questions you'd ask a breeder in their home – we discuss these in Chapter 5.

If you want a puppy from a breeder, all pedigree puppies will be registered with the Kennel Club in the UK, and breeders advertise their puppies on the site. This is a good place to start. Make a shortlist of 'possibles', then start phoning!

Another avenue to take is to look in the local newspaper. A pet owner may well adore their dog and desire just one litter so they can keep a puppy. Very often these people are the very best! They have read, marked, learned and inwardly digested everything they need to know about the care of their mother and ensuing puppies. But be prepared to ask all the questions we list in Chapter 5.

From a Home Breeder

If you can, visit a breeder for the first time when the litter is around four or five weeks old. It is unlikely (and frankly not desirable) that a breeder will allow you to see the litter before then as the mother won't be comfortable with strangers. You should look to take the puppy home at ideally ten to twelve weeks, and at least not before eight and a half, because a) the social fear period is between eight and ten weeks and b) he needs to learn social dog skills and communication from his mother and how to get on with other dogs through interaction with his siblings.

When visiting a home breeder, there is a lot to look out for. Most importantly, the home environment should be clean and comfortable, and the breeders welcoming and open, happy to answer all your questions – the answers to which should be at their fingertips (unless your questions are bizarre!).

The litter itself should be friendly and lively, interested and curious. If they are overly mouthy and bitey at six weeks, you know they haven't been handled well and it could turn into an issue (see page 80). Personalities show even at this young age, so there will always be the bold and assertive, and the shy and diffident, but there should be a general atmosphere among them of, 'Oh what's this then? New humans – let us have a look!' If *all* the puppies seem disinterested in you, lethargic or withdrawn: heed the warning bells. The only exception to this is if the puppies have just been fed and are sleepy, or if they have just emerged from a group game of rough and tumble. If the breeder tells you that this is the case, ask to come back in an hour or so – puppies recharge their batteries very quickly, so by then they should be raring to go!

Our preference is most certainly for a litter to be housed indoors, within sight and sound of the everyday workings of a human household. This way they become completely and naturally acclimatised to appliances such as vacuum cleaners, washing machines, television, radio, the doorbell – in fact, all the noisy objects and people which make up an average family home. If they are housed outside, these are sights and sounds which will have to be introduced to them at an age when they no longer accept without fear anything that seems to be part of their environment. They have begun to be aware, just as children do – and with that comes fear of the unknown, particularly when they have been removed from mother and siblings and are, for the first time in their lives, alone.

Housing outside is neither detrimental to their physical well-being (if the housing is of a high standard), nor (if they are well handled by humans) to their association with people. It just makes the transition to their new home a lot harder for them because they have not been socialised with the normal sights and sounds of a home environment. Before you start, they are on the back foot of the learning curve.

Ideally, if you have been able to see the puppies at four weeks, decided that you like what you see and have now gone back for one or several visits before making your final choice, you will have been able to see the personalities developing. This cannot always happen if you see puppies advertised at eight and a half weeks 'ready to go', but even then, try to make a couple of visits before making a final choice.

Many people say that their puppy chose them – it called to them, there was an immediate connection. We believe this instant, instinctive recognition of a kindred spirit is sound, and can be trusted, but if this does not happen, and if you are inexperienced, elderly or just want a quiet life, it would probably be best to look for your puppy in the mid-range of personality – neither too shy, nor too bold.

The next chapter gives more information on visiting a litter, what to look for and what to ask.

Rescue Centres

In the UK and all over the world, there are many unwanted litters of puppies. For litters being rehomed by a rescue centre, the puppies can have had a mixed bag of birth place experiences. Some owners will have been responsible. Their bitch became unexpectedly pregnant, but they looked after mother and puppies well, contacting the rescue when the pups were eight weeks of age for them to help find suitable homes. Perfect.

Of course you may come across pups born in the rescue centre, and without a doubt they will get lots of kind handling by the staff, so take a look at the litter and take all our points into consideration. With any litter, wherever born, if the mother is relaxed then the same will go for the pups. If she is stressed through pregnancy and beyond, this will result generally in stressed pups. Some rescue centres have staff who go above and beyond and will take a litter and mother home for the puppies to be raised in a home environment until they are ready for their 'forever' homes – this is ideal!

Others will have been brought in, at any age, when the owners decide they were too much work. These pups will have the trauma of being in two homes from birth already. However, at the rescue centre they will have had the opportunity of being cared for by kind human beings, and if very fortunate they may have been placed with a nurturing adult canine (like Patch). They'll have been kept fed and watered, and experienced warm, kind and gentle human touch. Hopefully, they won't have been overindulged with love and sympathy – they need empathy and this is very different. Empathy sees life from the point of view of the abused, and makes sensible inroads to make them feel understood and safe, so they can grow as individuals. By all means feel sorry for the puppy, but it is understanding and being confident and proactive – with love and guidance in equal portions – that will ultimately help them grow into well-adjusted adults.

Sometimes the puppy's parentage is dubious, so you may end up with a larger or smaller adult than you first expected. Make allowances for this. Can you afford him if he turns into a giant? Have you got the space? A rescue centre can give you a very rough idea of eventual size, but it's no guarantee.

We may not know what the rescue pup's early experiences were, but they certainly were not natural. These pups, along with ones that were fed and watered but taken away from their mothers at six weeks or earlier, start life on the back foot. However, I'd far rather take one from a rescue than hand over lots of money to a money-grabbing unscrupulous breeder, who may well think nothing of breeding again for financial reasons because we keep them in business.

Beware the Puppy Farm!

There is one rule here: *leave well alone*. Puppy farms come in all shapes and sizes, from those with many breeding bitches to those who just have a couple, but in all cases the care is poor or darn right cruel. Puppy farms and unscrupulous breeders use their breeding bitches as a money factory. When they get to six or seven years old, and have had the stuffing knocked out of them from multiple litters, they pass them on to rescues, unsuspecting individual dog lovers or maybe even put them to sleep. In our minds, three litters in any lifetime is enough for any bitch.

If Mum is not in evidence when you are shown the puppies, if the owner will not let you see *all* the puppies with the mother but insists on just bringing in the one *they* have chosen for you, be wary. At best they are control freaks, but more likely they do not want you to see the conditions under which the puppies are kept, their relationship with the mother or the mother's physical condition. The extreme end of this is that the puppies have either been shipped in, and the mother is languishing in a puppy farm at the other end of the country, or that the puppy has been stolen, placed with the facilitator and furnished with fake papers.

For the same reasons as above, *never* agree to meet a seller at a motorway service station, car park, in fact *anywhere* except the place at which the puppy has been born, where you can see its mother and siblings. The usual reason given for this kind of exchange is 'to save you the long journey'. The actual reason is that the puppy is a product of a puppy farm (which they would *not* want you to see under any circumstances) – or it is stolen.

It bears repeating, if the home is poor and you're not allowed to see the place the pups are being brought up in, walk away with very big strides. Call the RSPCA in the UK or ASPCA in the USA.

Puppy laundering

In recent years there has been a new breed of people engaged in 'puppy laundering'. These people import puppies from overseas and sell the pups on for profit. These puppies rarely have the appropriate vaccinations or have had any vets checks, and may carry forged papers which state they have. With the advent of pet passports (easily forged), these pups come from Europe and beyond and can carry any number of diseases, including rabies. Even if they do not, they are rarely in good health. If you do suspect a puppy is illegally imported, does not have a pet passport and is under fifteen weeks old, it may be in contravention of UK rabies legislation. Contact City of

London Animal Health and Welfare Team 0208 897 6741 or email veterinary.harc@cityoflondon.gov.uk or your local Trading Standards office (www.tradingstandards.uk/advice) to be put in touch with the animal health and welfare team.

The home puppy farm

The UK law allows a bitch to have six litters in a life time. The Kennel Club states:

> The vast majority of responsible breeders feel that this is too high and that there is potential for this to have a negative impact on the welfare of the bitch.
>
> Very serious consideration has to be given to the matter if a breeder wishes a bitch to have more than four litters, but the Kennel Club may grant permission for this to happen if it believes that there is good and justifiable reason for doing so on a case-by-case basis.

We have had recent experience of yet another type of unethical breeder – in essence, a small-scale puppy farmer in disguise. This one is harder to detect, but no less unpleasant. Lesley took a family member to see a litter of puppies – home bred, mother and father living with the puppies, socialised with children, only one breed of dog in the home. Perfect. Or was it?

This breeder had cleverly covered every 'usual' question. The puppies were regularly wormed, they had access to Mum, they had been vet checked, the parents had the correct certification (allegedly) for possible genetic disorders and KC generation pedigrees.

All fine so far, but in reality the puppies were kept in an outside garage, it was very cold, with only inadequate infrared lamps for heating. There were four adult dogs in the garden who were not allowed into the house. Although they obviously bred dogs for a living, there were no older dogs in evidence – what happened to them when their useful breeding days were over?

The pups were on newspaper over a concrete floor, and when we asked where the adult dogs slept, Lesley was told, 'Oh, in here with the puppies.' No beds, no bedding of any kind.

By the other wall of the garage, there was another bitch with two puppies – she looked very depressed and unconnected to her four-week-old pups. When Lesley asked how old she was, the answer was eighteen months – so this poor bitch was bred shortly after her first birthday. No wonder she looked unhappy and lost.

Lesley asked how many litters the mother of the puppies had produced: she was told 'two', and the mother was four years old. When she asked if this would be her last litter, they were astounded. 'Oh no, she can be bred until she is eight years old – but we only breed her once a year.' Unbelievable!

The worst thing was that when Lesley asked the opinion of her family member and potential puppy owner, she only said how cute the puppies were. She is not an unintelligent person; she just has little experience of dogs and breeders.

The British KC will not register litters from an overbred bitch – they have a maximum of four litters. But there is *nothing* the RSPCA could have done to stop this unscrupulous breeder. The dogs were not starved or beaten. They had shelter (of a kind). The puppies had been vet checked, wormed and fed adequately, yet the conditions under which all the dogs existed, and the agenda of these horrible breeders, was totally unacceptable.

Needless to say, they did not take a puppy.

By the way, the cost of these small terrier puppies? Nine hundred pounds each. A nice little earner if you have no conscience.

So be very aware, look beneath the 'perfect' credentials and judge by what you are seeing, not what you are told.

Online selling

You will find unwanted pets being sold on websites such as Gumtree. Many say it is because they have got divorced or are moving abroad. Whatever the reason, in our experience it is generally because the dog or puppy has problems, physically or behaviourally. If you want to go down this route, take a professional with you.

Caroline went to see one for a client who was unsure of the puppy he had found. The pups were advertised sitting on a soft fluffy sofa looking pristine. When visiting, Caroline was presented with a puppy who had gunky eyes, and was thin and lethargic. The sellers said he had just been fed and that's why he was so quiet, but it was clear from his stomach that he had not just been fed. He was shown without Mum and siblings, but when Caroline asked to see the others she discovered that mother was not allowed to be with her pups. She also had no visible teats, so Caroline was very sceptical that they were her pups at all. She asked to see the father and asked all the other delving questions . . . and knew when it was time to go when she asked to see the papers and they said she was asking too many questions. Caroline and her client left, and felt very uncomfortable indeed!

These pups were later advertised as not pure-bred pups, as in the first advert, but crosses – and looking at other adverts on the web there were more pups of different breeds, with a different name of owner, coming from the same place!

We believe that if people put puppies and dogs up for sale or rehoming on the web, at worst they are puppy farmers or the pups and dogs are stolen. At best, they are negligent and uncaring.

If your wish is to take on a pup who has had a bad start in life, if you have the time and even more patience and empathy, put your name down at the local dog rescue centre. He will be healthy, and you'll be helping stamp out unscrupulous breeding as well as giving a home to a little ball of fur.

CHAPTER 5
Visiting a Litter

As we said in the previous chapter, a good breeder will have their litters born and bred in the home environment, which should have a calm atmosphere, with well-behaved dogs and (if they have them) children. The puppies will have received careful handling from the owners several times a day since birth. They will be exposed to the normal movements and sounds within a family home under the protection and understanding of and their mother and humans, also the comfort of being together as a family with their siblings. This environment will produce a well-balanced puppy right from the start.

Socialisation starts from day one. It's not about getting out and about meeting and greeting a whole host of strange dogs, or over-loving people showering them with affection. Puppies need to know the feel of a loving human touch with no pressure. This should be done by the adults in the family, and children under strict supervision. Ultimately puppies will grow into dogs and will live with people. This time with his birth family – from zero to preferably ten to twelve weeks – is the most important in a puppy's life, and has a vital and lasting influence that can make all the difference between succeeding or failing in his new home.

We've seen puppies who have never been in a home environment, and they are scared of their own shadows; even the clink of a teaspoon in a cup is terrifying for them. They shake and bite to get clear of human touch. They find being on grass unusual and therefore house training becomes a struggle. We've seen it all, so if we sound alarmist it is because we have seen so much that we feel we must pass this knowledge on.

When you visit the mother and litter, stand back and watch the puppies all together. Don't lunge in there, just sit back and watch them playing and being together. If the mother is well balanced, and the puppies are around five to seven weeks old, then apart from a natural maternal watchfulness she should have no problems. If she is overly possessive, or the owners keep her away from you when you see the pups, or if she is lethargic and uninterested, then walk away – the puppy's personality will be in question. You want an easy-going puppy not a nervous wreck to contend with.

Personality is carried in genes, but the emotional state of the mother during the formative weeks will also have a big effect on the puppies. Too many litters starting at too young an age, living with humans who see her as a money-making machine, and therefore only provide the necessities of physical well-being without any emotional interaction, will make any mother withdrawn and depressed. Yes we humans can nurture, but nature and early conditioning also have a part to play.

Do not let your heart rule your head when choosing a puppy – yes, they are all cute! But you are choosing a lifelong friend who you want to be healthy in body and mind.

Puppies start shuffling around almost from birth, opening their eyes at around ten days, and their ears a little later (although they 'hear' by vibration from birth). At three weeks they become rather more mobile and at four weeks they are beginning the weaning process from the mother.

At five weeks their individual personalities are beginning to shine, and this is the best time to see the puppies. By all means meet the mum and observe the surroundings they are growing up in beforehand, if the breeder lets you, but do not expect to interact with them before four to five weeks. Before weaning commences interaction is not fair on the mother.

When you visit, the puppies should be bright-eyed with wet noses and clean soft coats. They should be very playful with one another and have a patient mother, who will from time to time tell them off if they put a paw over the boundaries of respect. There will be tumbling and some nipping, testing limits with each other. If you sit down, they may come to investigate you; the first one who ploughs in there maybe Mr or Mrs Bossy Boots. The ones that sit behind or are very tentative and showing signs of fear, leave alone; they will come in their own time.

A puppy that comes over and accepts a gentle stroke may be picked up. Gently hold him close to you, and massage. Lie him on your lap and hold his sides for support and comfort. If he struggles, let him go – he is not happy or comfortable. The one that stays for a gentle rub and relaxes with you is the one we'd choose. If they have had lots of kind touching from the breeders, prior to yours, they will more accepting of it from a stranger. Ideally, the breeders will have had their friends come in to handle the puppies early on, too, so you will not be such a novelty.

It can take many visits to the same litter (and often many others) to find the perfect puppy. Just because you want one now, do not go for the first puppy you see!

Paws for Thought

Lifting Up Puppy

Pick up a puppy by placing a hand under his bottom and the other hand between his front legs and hold close to your body. The closer you are to the ground the better. The closer they are held to you the better. Do *not* pick your puppy up by the scruff of the neck. Mothers pick puppies up by the body or head when they are small, and hardly ever resort to the scruff. It is not comfortable and certainly painful, and it is not necessary.

Questions to Ask

Do not be embarrassed to ask as many questions as you like. If the breeder is genuine he will not get annoyed with you. Quite the reverse, in fact. Speaking from experience, you'll find an unscrupulous breeder will get very irritated!

◆ Can I see the father? Be prepared to take time to travel, as he may be far away, but it's important to see he is a gentle lovable chap with no nervous or aggressive tendencies. Don't just take the breeder's word for it. If it's too much trouble for the sire's owners, then walk away.

◆ Can I see the pups with Mum?

◆ How old is the mother? How old was she when she had her first litter? How many litters has she produced? Bitches should not be bred before at least two years of age, and should not ideally produce more than four litters in a lifetime – and even then not in consecutive years.

◆ Are they vet-checked and can I see the report? Make sure you understand what you are reading and ask your own vet (see Chapter 14) for advice.

◆ Can I see their health certifications? The website www.dogbreed health.com has a very comprehensive and up-to-date list of all the vital tests that breed should have. It also has great information on what genetic diseases are carried by certain breeds, and much more. Ask to see the appropriate certification to show that both parents have been tested and found sound in these areas.

◆ Are they being toilet trained? Puppies should be taken outside after meals and when they wake.

◆ How often are they handled? If they have been handled well, when you hold a puppy at seven weeks he should be comfortable and relaxed in your arms.

◆ What are they being fed? A good natural diet would have us leaping and jumping with joy.

◆ How often are they being fed? Four times a day minimum from five weeks of age.

◆ Does the mother have access to her pups all day? She should be able to get in and out of the area with ease when she wishes, until they leave.

◆ Can I see the generations' pedigree? (If relevant.) If they are pedigree and not registered there may well be a perfectly innocent reason – on the other hand, the breeder may be hiding the fact that they have not been able to register the litter because either the bitch is too old or she has had too many litters, or that they do not want the world to know that they are breeding father/daughter/brother/sister or another too closely related combination. If you feel this to be the case walk away! There is the potential for the puppies to be burdened with many physical and mental issues that may not be highlighted until their older.

◆ What can you tell me about the puppies' different personalities?

◆ Finally, you should not have to ask, but wait to hear if the breeder says it – that they will take the puppy back for whatever reason and at whatever age. This demonstrates that they care more about the puppy's welfare than any financial reward.

Things to Look For

◆ Are the mother and pups well covered – i.e. with no ribs showing? There is no reason for either to be underweight.

◆ Bright eyes, no gunk!

◆ Wet noses.

◆ Clear and clean ears.

◆ Pink gums.

◆ Jaw straight so teeth meet at the front.

◆ Clean healthy coats; loose, supple skin.

◆ Clean floor and bedding.

◆ Solid motions. Soft or runny, they are either stressed or not being
fed the right food; or there is something medically wrong.
◆ Clean water available.
◆ That they are living in the house. The biggest most important parts
of socialisation are getting used to the normal sights and sounds of
family living. Your puppy will be living in your house, make sure
it was brought up in one.
◆ That they are living with Mum.
◆ Are the children and adults in the house gentle with them? Listen
to your gut feeling.

Paws for Thought

You must be prepared to wait for the right puppy. Do not
make rash decisions or buy on a whim. Your puppy
will be your companion for a very long time – it is
worth waiting for the right one.

You have now visited a few litters, and visited your chosen puppy
two or three times. Even if you think you have found the right one,
look at a few more litters and ask more questions to more breeders.
Then you'll be certain which breeder, litter and puppy best suits you.

Picking up your puppy should ideally be at ten to twelve weeks, and
certainly not before eight and a half weeks of age. Even if the breeder
tells you that you can pick it up earlier as you have had dogs before,
your puppy has never 'had a human' before and he will be missing out
on vital learning opportunities from his mother and siblings – it is not
fair and not necessary. Some may say that they bond better with their
human if they are picked up earlier. This is categorically not true! They
need their mother, and as long as they are getting great human interaction where they were born, staying with their mother and siblings in

a safe and familiar environment can only help them move forwards to becoming lovely well-balanced puppies. A breeder who insists it is fine should be walked away from, as it would make us really wonder why they had pups in the first place.

At six weeks they should still be occasionally on their mother's milk. Weaning only started at four weeks, and they only started crawling at two. Don't rush a puppy to be all grown up before he can. Their learning skills are amazing, but there is only so much stress the little body and brain can cope with. Too much pressure at too early an age can result before you know it in poor house training, diarrhoea, biting and over-the-top behaviour. Keeping stress to a minimum all starts with how the pup is socialised from birth in the home, and when and how you take him home.

CHAPTER 6

Preparing for your New Arrival

Timing is everything. Are you about to go on holiday? Are you about to have the kitchen refitted or have a baby? Is Christmas coming? Be realistic, and do not rush the decision to bring your puppy home. If the breeder insists you take him when convenient to them and not you, walk away – it is then not the perfect puppy for you. Think 'puppy' always.

Prepare Puppy's Room

Decide which room your puppy is best left in when you go out – many choose the kitchen. Make a bed space under a table, shelf, or in an open crate (see page 47 for more on crates). Get down on your hands and knees to see what's at their eye level. Are there possible dangers, like unprotected electric wires, small children's toys or cables for window blinds? Remove – or put on 'skyhooks' – anything which you do not wish to be investigated, so that when your puppy comes into his new home for the first time, you can allow him to investigate to his heart's content, without restraint and without you flapping, grabbing, saying 'No!' and generally creating an atmosphere of stress. His first impressions must be of calm and peace. Non-stressed humans are much more likely to be seen as viable decision makers than panicking fusspots!

There are many things you will need to buy for your home, too. Here is our list:

Food

Have a few days' supply of the food he has been fed on at the breeders. If it is a dry food, we suggest you move gradually on to a natural and biologically appropriate raw food diet (BARF for short). Diet is important to ensure your puppy grows strong and healthy in both body and mind. Dogs are primarily carnivores, and most dry dog foods are full of cereals and poor-value protein, which appear on the packet as 'meat derivatives' or 'meat meal'. This protein can be anything from feathers to tendons, or the left meat boiled off a carcass. Dogs naturally only eat 4 per cent naturally occurring carbohydrate – for example, berries – and most dry dog food has a good 40 per cent of carbohydrate used to bind the protein to a pellet. Quite simply, give your dog a natural diet and his behaviour will be normal and you'll have less visits to the vet. His poos will be much smaller and less smelly too, because his body is utilising a far higher percentage of the food. However, there are a few dry foods on the UK market now that are more holistic and appropriate to a dog's needs (see the Resources section for websites and books with more information).

Blanket

It is a great idea to give the breeder a square of blanket or towel a few day before you pick up your puppy, and ask them to place it in the puppies' bed. It will gather all the familiar smells of his mother and siblings, and when you bring the blanket home with your puppy it will help his transition by surrounding him with familiar smells.

Old towels

Have these handy for drying your puppy's feet and body each time he comes in from outside. It is important to do this even on dry days, so the puppy gets used to the idea that it happens always and gets accustomed to being handled in any situation. Feet can often be neglected during general grooming, so when you really need to do it he shies away and gets nippy.

Bed

Vet-bed type material is great; it is easily washed and dried and not easily chewed. Padded beds are likely to be ripped apart at an early age, and it's better to leave this investment until after teething – they'll just love pulling out the stuffing, and if the habit is learned young it will be difficult to sort out later.

Food bowl

Lift this up after each meal and wash ready for the next time. If your puppy seems reluctant to eat from his bowl, make sure that it is not the sound of his ID tag clinking on the bowl which is putting him off – replace with a soft plastic or rubber bowl. Less noise!

Water bowl

Keep full at all times, and as above.

Soft brush

For grooming.

Car crate – metal or fabric

When you pick your new puppy up, the best place to cary him is on your lap in the back seat, held gently and securely. But going forwards, it is very important to have a safe place for your puppy to be when in the car. A large car with a dog guard containing the space in the back is fine, too. Your puppy will travel better if he feels secure. If he shows concern with the cars whizzing past, either cover the crate or blank out the back windows.

You DO NOT need a handbag to put your puppy in!

This leaves your puppy with no choices but to put up with any situation, causing stress, anxiety and fear. Your dog is a sensate dignified being – not a fashion accessory.

Travel water bowl and bottle of fresh water

Keep these in the car, but change the water frequently.

Newspaper or puppy pads

Ideally, after each meal and every time the puppy wakes you will take him out for a pee. (Start using a trigger word, which he will come to recognise, and when he has performed give him a natural food reward.) However, every puppy is going to have the odd accident as his bladder is immature, so for these moments – when he is desperate and you haven't noticed – placing a piece of newspaper by the door is a great idea. If your puppy is having lots of accidents and not on the paper, soak a little of his urine on the pad and place by the door. This will help him get the message to pee there – dogs and puppies pee over old pee to replenish the scent. And, of course, when he pees elsewhere in the house, remember to clean up any pee with a biological cleaning fluid to destroy the enzymes and smell – particularly on carpet. This will have the effect of reducing the possibility of him marking/peeing in that spot again.

Collar and ID tag

By law all dogs need to wear these when outside the home, so your puppy will need to get used to it – we discuss how to introduce the collar on pages 74–6. Ensure his first collar is a soft one, and do not leave it on when the puppy is alone (or just with your other dog) as they can get hooked up on door handles, etc. You will find that having the collar on makes it is easier to guide your puppy, rather than taking hold of his skin, and so on.

The best ID tags in our opinion are made by www.ocpin.com. These fit close to your dog's collar and display a unique code. You record all your dog's details, from insurance to vets and medical conditions, in their database, and the bonus is you can add three contact names and details, and change contact details easily online if you go away for a weekend. Belt and braces for the microchip, which sometimes does relocate itself and is missed by scanners.

Microchip

In 2016 it becomes law in the UK that you have your dog ID microchipped, but it is a good idea to have your pup chipped anyway. Hopefully, it will become obligatory for all vets, police, rescues and so on to actually scan all dogs they deal with for microchips, too. When depends on the size of your puppy, so ask your vet's advice.

Harness

We do not advocate attaching a lead to a collar, or to have anything around the face of a puppy or dog. Both can cause harmful bruising to soft tissue of the skin and thyroid gland, and create skeletal and eye problems. If your puppy pulls, and generally he will if he is placed on a restrictive attachment, he will sustain untold damage that will manifest later in life. Instead, use a harness with wide, soft, supportive straps.

At six months, if you haven't managed to teach your puppy to walk with you with a loose lead, then it would be beneficial to move on to Caroline's carefully designed the Ultimate Happy At Heel Harness, which is available worldwide. It guides from the side and, if used correctly, will help you educate your adolescent from the word go to turn and walk and be with you. (See Resources for more details.) Most importantly, we suggest you start educating your puppy to follow you – it will come naturally from the beginning; you just have to nurture this desire in a low stimulus place, like home, and build up to busier places as able. Firstly, as we say, at home but *off* lead, and as a stress-free play lesson. We go into teaching this in more detail in Chapter 12.

Long training lead

For when you start going out and about.

Antler or bison horn chew

These are natural and great for teething. When your puppy latches on to your kitchen chair, you can guide him way – with no eye contact or speech – and give him the antler to chew. You're showing him, 'Don't chew that, chew this.' Avoid all cooked bones as the molecular structure changes, making them totally indigestible for canines, and they splinter and cause much harm and needless heartache for both you and your dog. Do not throw or have sticks to play with your puppy or dog. They again splinter, or in a moment of exuberance can get lodged in the teeth or worse still down their throats. Soak the antler in water overnight to make it a little softer for baby teeth.

Suitable safe toy

Choose ones that are safe and contain no detrimental chemicals, such as you find in rubber or plastics. One that is not easily ripped apart and is easily carried by pups, too. Do not leave toys with an unattended puppy.

Prepare your Garden

Spend some time (and money) ensuring your garden is escape-proof and safe. Make sure there is no sharp metal, glass or anything small enough – golf balls spring to mind – for an endlessly inquisitive and questing young puppy to swallow, chew or fall on.

Insurance and Vet

It is best to get these in place in good time before your puppy arrives. For insurance, make sure it covers each illness for life and not just for the first year he might have it. Word of mouth is the best way to find both.

Paws for Thought

We do not advocate using a lead attached to the collar. Use a soft back attachment harness to five or six months, then move on to the Ultimate Happy At Heel Harness to maintain a better bond when out and about.

Use Crates Wisely

Crates are something of an innovation of recent times, and at first the concept can appear to be rather unfriendly. However, if we stop thinking of them and using them as cages, they become rather less alarming – Sweden have passed a law to prevent the misuse of crates, and this indicates you must be wise about how and when to use one.

For dogs without issues, crates should be considered a refuge from the hurly-burly of a busy household – simply another form of bed that he is free to come and go in as he pleases.

For a dog with issues of past abuse, a covered crate can be hugely comforting as a place to which he can retreat, or a place where he can choose to go when you are unable to be with him, or when he wants some space. (But for traumatised dogs, it is massively beneficial for them to be with you most of the time, feeding off your unflustered and kind presence, whether they are on a lead or have physical touch, or are just calm and quiet.)

If he has become accustomed to a crate, when your dog *has* to be crated (for example, at the vets for a procedure, or for airlines and some ferry companies who require that he is put in a crate) it will not be a source of additional stress in an already stressful situation.

The single most important concern is that a crate should never be made a 'prison'. Do not use the crate to control your dog. The door should never slam shut, with all interaction at an end. It should be seen by your dog to be a relaxed and enjoyable place which belongs to him alone, and where no one will bother him. The crate door should remain open at all times, except when preparing for car travel and vets visits. Instead, take the time and trouble to calm your dog's over-exuberance, kindly and patiently, and show him how to become a relaxed and respectful member of your household. Using the crate as a prison is both cruel and lazy.

Make a place with good associations by playing 'come here' into the crate, rewarding with food each time. Take a minute or two, a few times a day each day, to play this. Feed your puppy in there too, door open. Practise with the door shut for seconds first, as at the vets and in the car they will have this experience and we don't want it to be stressful. Make sure the room you have your pup's crate in is safe and free from articles he can chew, apart from the toys he is allowed.

CHAPTER 7

The Journey Home

We recommend taking annual leave for your puppy's first two weeks. If you have children, make it a school holiday – but *not Christmas*! Even if there is someone at home for the majority of the day under normal circumstances, it is a good idea for the whole family to take part in the early days of bonding with your puppy, and you will all benefit from the relaxed atmosphere of 'holiday time'. There will be much less stress involved with the possible disturbed nights and constant dashing into the garden for poops and pees, and it's a good chance to establish, monitor and enforce the ground rules concerning interaction between your children and your puppy. It will generally give you time to observe and learn if you are not worried about work the next day.

This may seem like a lot of fuss, but it is far more desirable to create a situation where you have an excellent chance of getting things right from the beginning than it is to go in unprepared, cause a whole raft of issues and be forever firefighting the ensuing problems. At best, any unresolved issues will make your puppy a cause of tension and conflict with his human (and between humans), and create undesirable, stressful and permanent behaviour issues – not what you signed up for when adding a puppy to your happy family. At worst they can cause the dog to be sent to a rescue centre with a label around its neck, and a hugely compromised chance of a future happy life.

Having worked through Chapter 6, you will have already taken your new puppy's blanket to the breeder for his canine family to impregnate it with their comforting, familiar scent. You will have bought toys, bowls, puppy pads (or old newspapers), and made puppy's room safe and comfortable and your garden escape-proof.

If possible, arrange to pick up your puppy as early in the morning as the breeder will allow, so you will be able to spend the whole day gently introducing him to his new home and family.

There is no reason not to take the whole family to pick up your puppy (and your existing dog if you have one, see below) – but do ask them to stay calm and low key. Squealing children will raise the excitement level, and possibly the fear level too.

Make sure you take all you need from the breeder in the way of information: diet, worming and flea programmes, and a couple of days' supply of the food the puppy is used to.

It is most likely that you will be bringing your new puppy home in your car. Designate which adult will be responsible for holding the puppy on their lap before you leave home, to avoid arguments or indecision. This adult will need a couple of clean towels and something to clean up any potential vomit.

Carry the puppy quietly out to the car, seat the responsible adult, put the puppy on their lap, then get everyone else in – and just go. No chattering, no fuss, nothing to tell the puppy that getting into a car is anything but the most natural thing in the world. It is a real benefit if the breeder has taken the trouble to take the litter on short car journeys prior to your picking your puppy up, but if not, this will be the least traumatic way of introducing him to car travel.

Introducing your Existing Dog

If you are bringing your existing dog to pick up your puppy (and this is a good idea), give them some time to meet and greet each other before leaving the breeder's home. Ask the breeder to prepare an area where they can take each other in, off lead. Unlike with two adult dogs, you will not have had the facility to introduce pup and dog on any other neutral territory – the puppy should not have any vaccinations prior to twelve to sixteen weeks, as they would be rendered useless by the mother's antibodies still present within his system.

The alternative is to introduce them in the garden when you get home. This would probably be fine for most dogs, but if your dog is territorial (or even if he is not), suddenly finding a stranger in his garden may not fill his soul with joy.

Certainly this is perhaps a cautious 'belt and braces' method, but why not take every reasonable precaution available to you against the unexpected? You only have one chance to get this first meeting right.

Even if the two dogs seem to be getting on like a house on fire, do not put them together where your existing dog travels. Firstly, to be confined with a complete stranger is not any dog's idea of fun and, secondly, your new puppy has never travelled before (probably), so if he is nervous, the quiet security of your lap creates an immediate bond. Thirdly, he may well be sick, and your existing dog will not appreciate a heaving, vomiting, distressed travel companion – and you will not be able to clear up the puppy and the mess without fuss.

Paws for Thought
If Puppy is Sick

Be prepared for a journey with your new puppy and vomit! Clear it up without any fuss, bag and discard the mucky material in the footwell, re-seat the puppy on a clean towel, then gently massage his ears and neck – and apart from this reassuring touch, carry on as if nothing has happened. You will be showing the puppy that it has done nothing wrong, you are not angry and you have dealt with the mess. Think how you would react if a child was sick and then give your puppy the same gentle, non-judgemental treatment.

Remember, your puppy has been put into a noisy, strange, moving thing, which has taken him away from everything familiar, and to top it all he has been sick (and no one likes to be sick). An excited or blame-filled reaction at this early stage to something which he is already upset about can engender a fear of cars that can be very difficult to overcome.

When you arrive home, do not give in to the temptation to invite the whole world and his wife to share the joy of the arrival of the newest member of your family. For the first few days it should just be you and the people who will share his life on an everyday basis – keep everyone else away until he has settled in.

One Paw at a Time: Travelling Home

◆ Take a two-week holiday from when you pick up your puppy.
◆ Pick your puppy up from the breeder as early in the morning as possible, but after a good hour gap since his last meal.
◆ Take your existing dog with you if possible and introduce them in the breeder's home.
◆ Place puppy on an adult lap on the back seat of the car.
◆ Hold in a calm and relaxed manner.
◆ If puppy is sick, clean it up without fuss.
◆ Soft classical music in the car is fine, but don't boom out the latest rock hit.
◆ Bring home a puppy blanket that smells of his mother and siblings and a couple of days of his feed.
◆ Drive carefully!

CHAPTER 8
Arriving Home

When you arrive home, take the puppy straight into the garden. Neither mollycoddle nor abandon him. If he clings to your legs at first, just let him. Be a strong, comforting, silent presence. If he seems rooted to the spot, walk slowly around a little – he will go with you, and so the idea that being at your side is the best place to be ('walking to heel') is introduced in a natural and kind way.

Give him time to take in his environment and gather the courage to investigate. Do not 'encourage' him to explore, just allow him to go at his own pace. Think of a child on its first day at nursery. The children whose parents insist on them going to 'Play with the other children. Go on, don't be silly!' can end up as 'cling-ons' – children who hate pre-school – just because they were forced to interact before they were ready. If only the parents had the sense to let them take in their surroundings and decide for themselves when they wanted to join in and play, it would be *such* a different story.

The chances are that your puppy will take one look at the garden and launch into a frenzy of investigation and fun. This is the norm and, again, just let him get on with it and enjoy himself. Try to keep him out in the garden until he poops or pees – and then heap lavish, gentle, calm praise on him for the feat! You could get down to his level, and with a smile and a calm low voice say, 'Good puppy! We're so proud of you!' Make sure the praise is immediately *after* the 'deed' – if you praise when he starts, he may stop 'performing' and go to you. Don't suddenly bellow out loud an excited approbation (you can be enthusiastic without going wild!), or you will make him jump out of his skin and put him right off doing it the next time.

When he has had enough of the garden, call him into the house. If you all go in, calling happily for him to follow, he almost certainly will – and the first lesson in recall is established in a totally natural way.

Paws for Thought

It is very exciting for you to have a new puppy, but keep the atmosphere calm and conducive to settling in a stranger who has just left all he knows and loves.

Your house will have been prepared for his arrival, so let him investigate all the 'allowed' areas without interference – decide from the word go which areas will be no-go and stick to it, if he learns as a puppy he will accept it without question from that point on. If he pees or poops, do not make a fuss; just get one of the family to clear up while you take him back out into the garden and encourage him with whatever words you have decided upon (Lesley says 'Air your tail!'), to ask him to perform.

It will take some time for him to understand that the garden is the place to do his business, but start as you mean to go on. At first he will probably wander around the garden, do nothing, then come back inside and immediately perform! Keep calm, do not become angry. He is not trying to tick you off – he just does not yet understand where he is supposed to 'go'. Persevere.

Paws for Thought

When you want interaction with your puppy, call him to you and engage and give undivided attention. When you've

---

called him, don't make him sit when he arrives. What is the point? Some will say because it means he can't jump up, but you can simply show him that jumping is not acceptable by gently placing his paws back on the ground. Telling him to sit is just a lazy and non-empathetic way around the problem – and you've lost the recall lesson by failing to praise him for returning to you. In addition, making a dog sit time and time again is detrimental to his learning and to his physical health, as affirmed by the world-renowned behaviourist Turid Rugaas.

When he has thoroughly looked around, show him where his bed is. He almost certainly won't stay there at first, but soon he will realise that it is his 'safe' place, a place where, once he settles, no human will bother him. *Make sure that all the family understand this, and that they all respect his safe place.* You may favour a crate (door open), or a more traditional basket or duvet-type mattress, but whatever you choose, make the hard and fast rule that no one disturbs him when he goes to his haven, unless it is to sit quietly with him with a hand or leg for reassurance that he is not alone. Remember to put the blanket you picked up from the birth home in it, maybe a warm pad under it, too. Playing calm classical music may help him relax.

We all need peace and quiet sometimes.

Paws for Thought

Rest Time

Many dogs can relax when they are on their own. It's when their owners and other people appear that it all kicks off. You must give puppies time to relax and be themselves while they are in the same space as you, so that it's not all 'Go Go Go' when you are around. As puppies, if they are able to relax and sleep when all around them is getting noisy, then you will have a great base to start from. If they find it hard to switch off, it is because you have overstimulated them. Puppies need more gentle voice and massage, and less over-the-top play. They need choices to sleep away from you but be in the same space – a covered crate is ideal (with door open) or a bed under a table.

If you are allowing your puppy on the sofa or your bed, it is still a good idea to introduce him to his own bed first. This space is just for him, and will be his safe retreat. When you do introduce him to the sofa or bed, make sure it is always you who calls him over. He is too young to be able to jump up, so pick him up and place him next to you. When you want him to get down, call him to the edge of the furniture, pick him up and put him on the floor.

Dinner Time

Feeding should be a natural activity free from stress. At meal times, your puppy gets fed when he is quiet and undemanding. Eat a morsel of food yourself, such as a grape, then place the bowl down and turn away, but remain in the same room. Now he can eat in comfort, and enjoy.

If you ask your puppy to sit, it adds pressure. If you stare at your puppy, you are indicating that you may reclaim the food. By eating a morsel and turning away you will show, in the only way that dogs understand, that you have eaten your fill and the rest is his. Dogs do this naturally to each other, so why not take a leaf out of their book and do likewise.

One Paw at a Time: Arrival Day

◆ Pick your puppy up from the breeder as early in the morning as possible, but after a good hour' gap since his last meal.

◆ When home, keep calm and quiet, and do not overload the house with people, noise and parties. In fact, at first he should meet no one except those he will be living with permanently.

◆ Take him straight into the garden to pee and poop. Calmly reward when he has performed.

◆ Don't force him to go and play. If he is stuck to your leg, slowly walk around the garden.

◆ In his own time, let your puppy investigate his new home, first the garden, then his 'allowed' areas in the house, making sure that the 'no go' areas have been made inaccessible.

◆ Show him his bed, under a table or in an open crate covered with a blanket, in the kitchen preferably, and place the blanket he had with his litter in there.

◆ Feed him close to his bed when he has had time to sniff and familiarise himself with the kitchen, bed and garden areas. Then try taking him out again to have the opportunity to pee and poop.

◆ Call him to you for gentle strokes, massage and cuddles, but do not force the issue if he just wants to relax in his bed or is simply relaxing on the floor because he is tired. Keep it calm and low key.

◆ After about two hours, if not before, he will need a sleep. If you keep everything calm on arrival, and don't gee him up to play, he will be able to do this. Encourage him to use his bed, but at this stage don't insist.

◆ Have no visitors for a couple of days, so the puppy can find his feet with you and investigate his new surroundings. He is not your latest toy, and needs time to adjust and feel secure – it's all new, everything is different, no familiar sights, sounds or smells. You have all the time in the world. Do it slowly and you'll do it right and not freak your puppy out.

◆ There is no need to push play yet; he needs to take so much in that it will fry his brain.

◆ Don't let him jump up on the furniture, it is bad for his growing body. If he is allowed up, call him over and lift him. And the same again for getting down.

◆ Children should be gentle and kind. Teach them that his is a living being, not a toy.

◆ A little of everything is good. Don't overdo it. And above all, keep the environment calm. Do not rev your puppy up to overexcitement and overstimulation. He needs a relaxed life with calm and gentle humans.

◆ Do not pressure him to be the centre of attention.

CHAPTER 9

The First Few Nights

You have now spent the day with your puppy and hopefully all has gone swimmingly, but now comes the dreaded moment when you all go to bed . . .

Remember, this is the first time in his little life that he has spent any time away from his mother and siblings. Hopefully you have given him time to feel safe and investigate his new surroundings, and he has had sleep and massages and cuddles at times throughout your well-thought-out day, so until now he has not been too homesick and upset or stressed – either with too much play or from missing siblings and Mum.

All that will go out of the window if he finds himself alone in the dark without his family, or his new friends.

Paws for Thought

Your puppy is feeling alone and sad and missing his home. Be understanding, but do not overdo the love and attention to compensate. Be thoughtful in your approach to settling him into your home.

So how do you help him get through his first night?

The traditional approach has been to start as you mean to go on – in other words, let him howl the house down. Of course he *will* eventually get used to being alone at night, but it's not very pleasant for him, is it?

One Paw at a Time: Puppy's First Few Nights

◆ We advocate spending the first few nights alongside the puppy. If he is to sleep in your bedroom, move his bed next to yours. If he is to sleep in the living room, move his bed next to the sofa, where you will need to spend a few nights.

◆ When you all go to bed, each time he whimpers or whines, just put your hand down on to him. This no-fuss contact is reassuring.

◆ Gradually move his bed further away each night, until it is in the place you have chosen for him to settle quietly (and in time, alone) in his safe place. You have gently helped him to adjust, over the first few nights, to a new place with new smells. If he is really lucky he'll have an older dog to snuggle up to and all should be well.

One Paw at a Time: Puppy's First Few Nights in a Separate Room

◆ If it is your preference to have him sleep in another room, make sure that all your preparations for bed are done first.

◆ Settle your puppy in his bed, with a warm low-voltage purpose-made warm pad or warm hot water bottle, a toy and the blanket infused with the scent of his mother and siblings.

◆ Have soft music from Lisa Spector playing (www.icalmdog.com) and rest your arm on him.

◆ Then simply turn out the lights.

◆ Don't speak, but an ear massage may go down very well.

◆ When he is sleeping, stay a while fiddling around the room quietly or drinking your last cuppa before bed, then leave when your pup remains asleep.

◆ Leave the soft music playing to give the room some sign of life. He should be tired after a day of change and ready to sleep.

◆ . . . Until (of course) he finds himself alone for the first time in his life! Almost certainly he will cry then. Go back in, pick him

up and put him gently back in his bed, without speech but with ~
gentle stroke and brief kind eye contact.

◆ Sit with him and preferably sleep with him, then turn out the light again.

◆ If you have decided not to sleep with him, leave when he is asleep but be prepared to continue this over the coming hours and nights.

◆ You will probably have to do this quite a lot for the first few nights, but persevere, because he *will* eventually realise (and accept) that his place is in a different room from you at night. By you reappearing in a calm and unfussy way when he starts to become hysterical, you are reassuring him that he is not abandoned – just that you have decided that he is not going to have your company at night.

Teaching a puppy to sleep alone is a heartbreaking thing to do, and if you have a lone puppy or dog it is always best to have them sleep with you. But unfortunately there is no getting around the fact that in many cases dogs and humans sleep in different rooms. Most puppies accept this separation fairly quickly – especially if you work on building the bond and trust from the word go, and keep days calm, especially the time running up to bedtime.

Of course, if you have an older, well-balanced dog, who has shown himself to be happy with the newcomer, then your job is done for you! Your new puppy will almost certainly settle happily near his surrogate canine parent, and you can go to bed.

The wonderful thing about dogs is that once you have gained their trust, love and respect, you are their world, and incapable (in their eyes) of making a duff decision. Great for your ego, but your responsibility is to be the great decision maker they have decided you are – and to give them the calm leadership which ensures that you live up to their image of you.

No pressure, then!

Paws for Thought: Do Dogs Like Cuddles?

Many dogs do not like close face contact or tight cuddles even with their owners, and certainly not with strangers. It is not natural for them to be stuck in a situation that disables movement, and therefore restricts them and forces them to look straight into the eyes of another.

Does your dog lick or pant or turn his face away from you when you hold him this way? That means he isn't happy. It's the same as a child turning their head and pushing away when they are thrust into someone's arms to say hello.

Children go to cuddle puppies and grab them round the neck in a tight embrace – does your dog nuzzle in or turn his face away, straining his neck? Be wise and watch what your dog is telling you. It only takes once for us to get it wrong and the puppy be blamed for something that he was forced to react against.

Dogs don't meet eye to eye, and we shouldn't expect them to embrace us as we expect our other nearest and dearest to. They are dogs we are humans. But also remember that we humans wouldn't want a tight disabling embrace from anyone we only know in passing, either.

CHAPTER 10
Your Existing Dog and the New Arrival

Your existing dog (or dogs) will hopefully accept his new housemate, if not with delight and joy then with calm resignation. He may be very excited to have a new chum, and follow him around trying to persuade him to play (the puppy will almost certainly be too busy exploring to engage . . . *yet*!), or he may hold himself aloof, deliberately turning his back and refusing to interact at all.

Both reactions are fine.

Do not be tempted to force the friendship – do not interfere and do not react. Allow the dogs to acclimatise to each other in their own canine way.

Although an older dog 'telling off' a puppy can sound quite violent and the puppy will undoubtedly squeak and squeal, it is appropriate behaviour. The puppy is not being hurt. In a flash, the puppy learns a valuable lesson in manners and all returns to normal in seconds, except that the puppy will show more respect to the older dog – just as it should.

The only exception is if your existing dog becomes too 'unfriendly', and all isn't back to normal within seconds. If this happens, remove yourself and the puppy from the older dog's space. It is far better for the older dog to approach the younger one in his own time. Unfriendliness will never (at this early age) come from the puppy.

If the older dog is being harassed by the puppy, use puppy-appropriate methods to remove him from the situation – distract him by turning away, showing him something more interesting to play with, or just turn him and hold for calm. When he leaves the older dog alone or approaches with respect, then all is good and sorted.

Problems arise if you decide to jump in to 'protect' the puppy by telling off your older dog. This means the puppy learns he can torment the older dog with no comeback – because you have stopped the older dog retaliating or, more precisely, being able to defend himself. The puppy is well on the way to becoming a thug, and the older dog feels attacked but unable to protect himself. He will become withdrawn and miserable.

Take control of the situation calmly, and with quiet authority – show both dogs that you are the decision maker, and that you will not tolerate bullying from the older dog or bugging from the puppy.

It is important to keep an eye out for over-the-top reprimands from the older dog, but other than that, please let them get on with it – they understand each other better than you ever will!

Paws for Thought

It can be a shocker having a new playmate 24/7 if you've only ever been a solo dog. It can take time to readjust.

Once the two dogs have established their relationship (and it will be at least a relationship of tolerance from the older dog until the young whippersnapper stops being irritating and starts being a chum!), your older dog will teach canine manners and etiquette in a way that we humans can only dream!

Do not be tempted to 'pander' to your existing dog because you feel guilty for introducing a puppy. Remember you are the decision maker and it is your duty always to do what is best for the dogs in your care. You will, by your actions, show your existing dog that the new puppy is not an issue for him. You won't take away the affection he has enjoyed as an 'only' dog, nor will his place in the home be usurped.

You won't, in any way, compromise the safe and secure life he has led since electing you to be his decision maker.

Show him that nothing has changed in your relationship with him and he will completely accept, and understand, the softer and age-appropriate way in which you interact with the puppy.

The most important thing to remember is that, at this early stage, your puppy is like a sponge. He will soak up everything. So make sure that your mind is calm and your body language confident and reassuring. If he sees you dealing with every aspect of his new environment, including the creatures that inhabit it, with total authority and without fuss or fear, not only will he take from this that he need not be afraid, but also that you are the person best suited to follow when he is unsure.

CHAPTER 11

Acclimatisation at Home

First and foremost, socialisation and acclimatisation in the first couple of weeks is about settling in, feeling comfortable with the inhabitants, both human and animal, of your puppy's new home. He needs to feel happy and safe with all that is going on in the home and garden – beyond comes later. This will be pretty straightforward if the puppy was brought up in a home environment with all the usual noises, sights and smells of daily living.

Between eight and ten weeks the 'social fear' period is occurring. Again, it is useful to compare a similar stage in human child development.

A baby (and later a toddler) has complete trust in his parents – he has no fear at all of anyone or anything, but then comes the time when he has moments of being shy or self-conscious, or fearful of a new experience. He is beginning to become self-aware, and all parents know how carefully this stage must be handled. One wrong move can cause an aversion to a person or situation which can last a very long time.

Your new puppy is going through the same self-awareness stage, and needs to be handled as carefully as you would a child. Introduce new situations calmly and sensitively, and be very aware of your puppy's body language. If he shows fear or even nervousness in a new situation, or meeting a new human, back off and show him that you will never force him into situations before he is confident.

'Social fear' is an ongoing process. Our child encounters so many new situations and people in the 'growing up' stage – experiences which can either be accepted and embraced with the help of a sensitive parent, or can become source of discomfort or even fear, and this mindset sometimes follows them into adulthood. Your puppy is essentially no different.

How you address the smallest things will have a bearing on how your puppy will be to move forward into becoming a happy well-adjusted adult dog.

Personality has a huge bearing on coping with different experiences, but remember, whatever the personality, it is what you *do* in response to your puppy's reaction that is important, not what you say. Unless they have a medical issue, puppies are neither born aggressive nor 'naughty'.

Paws for Thought

Puppies are not born aggressive. It is *how* you socialise and *who you socialise with* that is important to prevent nervous or assertive personalities. Puppies turn into aggressive dogs because of inappropriate or badly managed socialisation.

Puppies need to find out about and acclimatise to their new environment – and they need to do it in the way puppies do. If they can't reach, they will jump up. If they want to test objects, they will put them in their mouths and chew. If they want your eye contact, they will (again) jump up to get your attention. They may bite, and in doing so learn how hard they are allowed to bite. If they are extremely nibbly and bitey, you can reasonably conclude that they had very little gentle human interaction before you got them. If something runs away, they chase, or growl or yap, or they may cower – or pounce. It is all about finding their feet, and fitting in. They were not born with a rule book – and they certainly were not born human.

They will become socially acceptable members of our society if we socialise and acclimatise them to each new experience slowly, and keep taking note of how they are accepting the situation. If they want out from a new encounter, take them away to a greater distance – better still, start off at a greater distance and work forwards and backwards, each time getting closer, then passing. This takes time, and not necessarily only one session. When encountering new situations, they first need to learn you are there for them and understand their concerns. You need to do what is right so they know you know. With this grows trust and love and the best bond you could ever wish for.

As our puppies grow up they need to be sociable with people and dogs, and acclimatise to cyclists and cars – in fact all of the sights and sounds of our busy world. They need to know that there is always someone they can trust leading the way and supporting them in making the right choices.

The way we socialise is of great importance. Puppies will only turn into nervous man- or dog-eaters if forced into situations that make them feel vulnerable – when they are forced to socialise with people and dogs who are manner-less.

They will only attack, lunge or bark at cars, bikes, vacuum cleaners, mowers, etc. if they were originally introduced to these things in the wrong way – in a way which caused them fear and distress.

Watch his responses to what he is seeing, smelling and hearing, not only to the object to which you wish to accustom him, and also be aware of *your* response to him. If he does not respond in the way you wish and you sound grumpy, he will translate this as you sounding and feeling anxious about what was bothering him. You will be feeding his fear and making him believe that he was right to be afraid.

Dealing with New Experiences

There will be a lot of new experiences in your puppy's first few days. Comforting with words, cuddling and generally fussing is natural to us when we see a vulnerable creature in fear, and we have the very best of intentions, but it sends entirely the wrong message to your puppy.

Even with children this approach can be inappropriate in certain circumstances. Think of the first time your child experiences a thunderstorm. You have one of three ways of reacting:

1. You dive behind the sofa, dragging the child with you and saying, 'Oh, I hate thunderstorms too – I *think* we'll be safe here!'
2. You tell the child not to be wimp, face his fears and, 'Don't make such a silly fuss – it can't hurt you, so stop being so stupid.'
3. You say, 'Oh, a thunderstorm, how exciting! Let's go to the window and take a look. We can count the seconds in between the flashes and bangs to see how close it is – then if it is still raining, shall we go into the kitchen and make those little cakes Grandad likes, until it stops and we can go outside again?'

We think it's clear that number 3 is best!

Obviously you cannot speak to your puppy in the way you can your child – and nor would it be desirable in times of stress. Words mean little to a puppy; they distract his focus from your body language (which is a canine's main way of reading another creature) and often convey a state of stress. When you are either correcting behaviour or in a worried frame of mind, it is far better to remain silent. Show by your body language that you are not reacting because you have decided that there is nothing to fear, and that you can be trusted to deal with anything life throws at you and you will keep him safe. Then he will decide that there is nothing for him to fret about.

Make nothing out of something – and never make something out of nothing.

Paws for Thought

Do not get your puppy to sit and 'face his fears'. By doing this you are disabling his own natural body language and being a control freak! Don't do it. Walk him away from fears and keep him moving, so his focus is on what you are doing, and not on the object which has caused him fear.

Household Appliances

If you drop a pan, or there is any loud and unexpected noise, do not make eye contact or make a verbal or physical fuss. This would show your puppy it's a big deal.

Instead, pick up the pan, and if your puppy is cowering give him a brief and comforting touch, or divert his attention to something else for a moment.

Fear of the vacuum cleaner is one we come across frequently, but you can use this technique with whatever item your puppy is worried about.

When a working vacuum is first introduced to a puppy, the shock can result in frantic chasing and barking. Unfortunately, this can be interpreted by the humans as a hilarious new game for your new chum, and the sight of him chasing – all ungainly puppy legs going like pistons – is 'so funny and cute'. It's not quite so funny in the months to come when the appearance of the vacuum sends him into a frenzy of chasing, barking madly trying to bite it – or if it causes him to panic and dive for cover.

One Paw at a Time: Introducing Puppy to the Vacuum Cleaner

This advice is for the vacuum cleaner, but can equally be applied (with appropriate variations) to any other noisy or moving item used within the house or garden – lawnmowers, washing machine, broom, etc.

◆ Always begin vacuuming in a room a distance away from where the puppy is.

◆ When you reach his room, place yourself between puppy and appliance. Give the pup an exit so he can remove himself.

◆ Keep an eye on your puppy, and if he sinks down, eyes wide or licking lips, ears to the side, then you should stop. He is using signals of calming – he's not happy and the experience is too much.

◆ The cure for this is desensitisation. Have the vacuum in a room without switching it on, so it will just become another ornament. Do not look at your puppy for a reaction; just be very matter of fact and have yourself between the vacuum and the puppy.

◆ When the puppy accepts its presence, without fear or excitement – this can take days – move it to another position.

◆ When your puppy is happy with this, start to move it around the room without switching it on. Continue in this vein to the logical conclusion of using the vacuum as it is intended.

◆ At each stage *stop* when your dog shows signs of stress, or preferably before. Everything must be accomplished slowly, and do not move on to the next step until your dog shows that he is completely comfortable with the previous – showing no signs of yawning, licking lips or stretching.

◆ If you try to rush the process you will end up back at the beginning. You must keep calm and controlled at all times, and do not try to comfort your dog when he reacts (that will just convince him that he was right to react) – just stop, walk away from the cleaner and quietly engage in another activity.

◆ It can be a slow and frustrating process, but you will get there in the end.

For more information on signs of stress, see Brenda Aloff and Turid Rugaas books in the Resources section.

Paws for Thought: Dogs and the Law

Get savvy on your dog law for your country. In the UK, you can now be prosecuted if your dog is perceived to be threatening, or even intimidating, whether in your home or garden, or outside. How this can possibly be implemented is a moot point, as if your dog should meet a person who is very nervous of the canine species, an over-exuberant greeting could be deemed threatening. So, not only must your dog have perfect manners, he must be seen to have perfect manners. It is up to you to make sure he is never put in a position where he feels the need to defend himself – that is your job, and if you are not diligent it will be he who pays the price.

Visitors to your Home

Most people are excited about a cute new puppy, and you have managed to hold wider family and friends off for a week or two. But now that your puppy has settled into your home, and he is beginning to accept and bond with the people with whom he will live, how should you introduce him to your friends?

When someone enters your house, the first thing they will do is look down at the puppy. However, eye-on-eye contact isn't something that seems welcoming to a dog, and this will cause your puppy some concern. This is when stressy jumping up and peeing on the floor can begin. Instead:

One Paw at a Time: Introducing your Puppy to Guests

◆ When visitors arrive, he may well bark or indicate their presence in some other way, like running to the door. He's doing a great job, but now this is your signal to take over.

◆ Acknowledge him with a word in an assertive but friendly manner. You can say anything from 'thank you' to 'bananas', as long as you always use the same word. Call him to you.

◆ Guide your puppy behind you when people enter. If your door opens directly onto the street, it is wise to attach a lead to puppy for safety – then guide him behind you.

◆ Ask your guests to look and talk to you, so that your pup has a chance to sniff and investigate. He doesn't want a cuddle from a stranger, he wants to find out about them.

◆ If he jumps up at them, just guide his paws down or gently walk into him. You do not want him to become the demanding centre of attention.

◆ When your visitors have been sitting down for a while, and your puppy is relaxed with their presence – and better still, has pottered off – then one guest can be invited to call the puppy over.

◆ Your guest should crouch, making themselves smaller and lower, so your pup will feel happier with the invitation.

◆ If he comes, your guest should make it a gentle encounter of strokes and massages, with calm gentle vocals.

◆ Do not force an interaction; if your puppy is not interested then let him be.

◆ The more people visit, the more your puppy will feel confident in coming to them when they call. Do not pressure him, just as you wouldn't pressure a child to get close and personal with a stranger.

◆ If the pup becomes jumpy or mouthy, ask your guest to stop their interaction.

◆ Then calmly step in and hold the pup and carry on talking to your visitors.

◆ If he continues to be mouthy, simply give him something he can chew and stop the interaction. If each human's interaction with him is calm and gentle, this is far less likely to occur.

Paws for Thought

Dogs and puppies should be given every opportunity to be canines. If the act doesn't fit into our world, then guide the dog to act in a way that is acceptable. For instance, bottom sniffing is a way canines find out about their peers; it is a polite, 'Hello, who are you?' So if this is done to a human, don't shout and get embarrassed as they are just doing what nature tells them. All you have to do is gently guide them away without a word. They are trying to find out about new visitors, so let them sniff, but not there!

Collars, Harnesses and Leads

It is likely that your new puppy has never worn a collar, or felt the restriction of a lead and harness, so the introduction of these three unnatural, but for our world essential, pieces of equipment must be carefully thought out.

If you are carelessly unobservant you could be storing up a world of stress for both of you. Be proactive in watching and reacting to your puppy's response to these alien items being attached to him. Make sure you are not heavy handed.

There is no rush for the first collar. Wait until you feel that you have started to bond with your puppy, that he is beginning to trust and feel comfortable with you, and that he is relaxed and settled (without his mother and siblings) in his new home.

Some puppies accept the feel of a collar around their neck with absolute sangfroid, and others react like an unbroken horse in a rodeo – be prepared for either!

One Paw at a Time: Introducing the Collar, Harness and Lead

◆ The first collar should be soft and easily fitted.

◆ Slip it on as part of a caress, and before your puppy has time to react. Use distraction tactics, giving food rewards as you put it on; you are then making a great association!

◆ Immediately, call him to play gently with you some more – whatever he enjoys, do it. A massage will probably do the trick.

◆ He may well just accept the collar without fuss and not really notice it, but if he shows that he is very aware of an alien presence around his neck, make the association for him that the collar and something fun happen simultaneously.

◆ If he responds, enjoy the game.

◆ Then, when all is calm and he suddenly discovers that he does not approve of the thing around his neck, call him to you, give him a quiet treat and a gentle massage. He will enjoy the relaxing stroking.

◆ Hopefully he will drop off to sleep, and when he wakes, the collar will no longer be something new and irritating to him.

◆ If your puppy finds it stressful, easy does it. Day by day, call your puppy to you, give him treats and loving contact and a gentle massage, and then put the collar on when you don't have to force the issue. Do it in his time, not yours. It will probably be several weeks before you are able to go out into the world anyway, so there is no hurry.

◆ When he is completely comfortable with his collar – in other words, does not even seem to know he is wearing it – you can start to introduce the harness in the same way.

◆ And then, when he is completely happy with his harness and collar, continue by attaching a long lead to the harness. There are instructions for this on pages 89–91 in Chapter 12.

Paws for Thought: The Harness

We strongly advise you do not use a lead attached to a collar or face harness. For a young puppy, use a soft-back attachment harness with padded breast plate. At six months, the side attachment Ultimate Happy At Heel Harness designed by Caroline is perfect for your puppy's physical and mental well-being.

Once your puppy has discovered a fear of the collar, you face an uphill struggle to reverse his reaction – much better to go slowly, using his response as your guide to how quickly (or slowly) you should go to achieve a result. You can start playing Follow Me off lead very early on. Don't venture forth to the outside world on a lead until you have thoroughly prepared the ground.

Other Early Lessons

Introducing massage and grooming

You can massage your puppy from day one. Do this gently and soothingly, and gradually increase the time you spend massaging him all over, slow but sure. Include the head, legs, paws, jaws, back, legs, bottom, and tail and ears. Julia Robertson gives some great techniques in *The Complete Dog Massage Manual* (see Resources).

When your puppy is enjoying your massage sessions, you can introduce a soft brush. Again, do this gently and for short periods of time. Make this initial 'brushing' a form of stroking. Give your puppy no reason to see the brush as something which pulls or scratches, or in any way a less than enjoyable experience. Most puppy coats need little grooming – it is only when they grow their adult coat that it is necessary to be more vigorous – so ensure that your puppy is fully familiar and comfortable with the grooming process, and he will accept more intense grooming with equanimity later on. It is the same with bathing. We suggest you go to your local pooch parlour – watch how they do it and get a lesson on grooming.

If your puppy is happy with both these human interactions, when he needs to be restrained in the car or at the vets later on he will already be used to being held.

Teaching patience

We all have to learn patience. It cannot be forced upon us, we learn by example.

One Paw at a Time: Patience at Home

Your puppy may be the centre of your universe, but you don't want him to be so dependent on you that he can't be without you – just as we teach children independence, so they can rest and play on their own as well as with us. It's a good thing.

◆ When you enter a room, say a brief hello and then concentrate on your own task. This introduces the notion that your puppy is not the centre of the universe. You're not ignoring your puppy, but you are delaying interaction and teaching respect and patience.

◆ If he jumps up, simply place his paws down on the ground, If he tries to make this into a game, gently take a step towards him so he naturally ends up on four paws. No eye contact or vocals, so that you do not give him attention for undesirable behaviour.

◆ When he has stopped demanding your attention, so he's in your vicinity but not pestering, then, if you wish, you can call him to you. He gets you on your terms. He is learning patience and the beginning of recall.

This technique stops mugging when you come into a room. It prevents attention-seeking behaviours, and gets the puppy to think about you and your needs – not just him and his wants!

Doorway manners

When you try to leave a room, if your puppy barges past you he is showing no respect whatsoever for personal space. As he gets bigger, it will become more problematic. Here is the way to avoid this:

One Paw at a Time: Teaching Respect of your Personal Space

◆ If your puppy barges past you, shut the door between you and him.
◆ Leave it shut for five seconds then open again, stand back, and don't look down or call him back into your space. Your puppy will reappear as if by magic.
◆ The next time you open the door, he will take note of you. He's watching to see if you are going to go through or not.
◆ He will stand back respectfully and let you walk through, and then follow naturally.
◆ When he has done so, heap huge praise on him. He's made you very happy, so he'll be happy, too.

However, a few puppies find this a great new game. They will run through, wait for you to reopen the door, and run through again – great fun! If you have a puppy like this, use a slightly different strategy:

◆ Open the door a crack; the puppy will lunge to get through.
◆ Shut the door, and gently manoeuvre your puppy behind you.
◆ Repeat, opening the door a little wider each time, until you are standing in front of the open door, with your puppy waiting respectfully for you to go through first.
◆ First to last, do not speak at all!

◆ Play this game on inside doors, as they are infinitely easier. As with all lessons, they should be short and carried out in a light-hearted fun manner and the lesson will be learned.

By teaching your puppy these manners you will prevent him growing up to be a 'barge past' bully.

Do not say wait and sit, then call him, or all you have taught is the trick of control. It needs it to happen naturally, so your puppy will learn respect, patience, and how to watch and learn.

Dogs naturally stand back for those who they respect in the canine world, and so do we in our human world. Teach this as a matter of course and it will make your life so much easier.

Paws for Thought
No!

The word 'No' has a very negative feel, and has the effect of making you sound, and feel, cross and aggressive. It is also meaningless to your dog. On the one hand, he has got your attention for doing the wrong thing, which could mean it will turn into an attention-seeking behaviour. But on the other it also comes with a grumpy look from you. This can crush a dog as much as physical reprimands.

There is no place for the word 'no' if it's always given in a grumpy fashion. However, a single loud shout from you in an emergency situation (like running towards a road) will be effective. As it is so out of character for you, the pup will turn, and then you call and run away, beckoning him to follow.

If you use a loud shout for all the little things that really can be dealt with in a very much more imaginative and compassionate way, then it's a word they learn to block and fear.

Mouthing, nipping and biting

All puppies mouth and puppies bite, but they have to be taught it is not acceptable. Mouthing is a gentle investigation of items or people. Bite inhibition is first learned when in the litter – but primarily where it concerns other canines. A puppy that bites a sibling too hard will lose the game in which he is trying to engage the other puppy. The bitten puppy removes himself and the game ends – no fun for the biter, so he learns. The other scenario is that the puppy being bitten turns and latches on to the biter, hurting him as much as he is being hurt – this is also no fun for the original puppy, so he learns.

When your puppy is old enough to play with others, you will see that all canines play robustly, often using their teeth, but the lessons learned in their litter days ensure that the 'biting' never reaches the stage where it hurts. If this happens inadvertently the bitten dog will react either with a yelp, or retaliation, and the fun stops immediately. A well-balanced dog that has (usually through overexcitement) overstepped the mark, will react to this 'telling off' with appeasing behaviour, and no further escalation occurs.

With humans a puppy must learn that 'teeth on skin' is never acceptable, and we do this in the early days by yelping, turning away, and immediately withdrawing ourselves. If you react angrily, or with retaliation, you are buying into his mindset, and this is not useful at all. You should address all instances of mouthing so it does not escalate to nipping or biting.

One Paw at a Time: Mouthing and Nipping

◆ So far as sleeves are concerned, don't wear floppy sleeves!
◆ If your puppy has taken hold of your sleeve or trouser leg while in the throes of a cuddle or play, remove his mouth and say nothing. Carry on stroking gently.

◆ If he repeats, remove his mouth and walk away. This is what his siblings would do when a game becomes too rough or they find the game to be no fun.

◆ It is neither necessary nor desirable to isolate the puppy in another room or to walk out of the room. He is not biting in the aggressive sense: your puppy is just learning what is, and is not, acceptable when playing. You are just saying that if you nibble at clothing, the game or interaction ends.

◆ When he potters off to do something else, call him for a cuddle or massage immediately. This shows him that he gets your attention on your terms, and the bonus is that it has given you a great opportunity to do some recall work.

◆ If your puppy continues in the same behaviour, he is probably too tired and overstimulated to take in your signals, and needs rest time. This is when he needs to be shown to his bed for self-soothing time. Please stay in the room, but give him a chance to sleep without the pressure of looking at him and telling him to sleep. Have some gentle music playing. (Puppies, like children, need to learn to sleep when all about them are carrying on doing their normal daily routines. The sound of you pottering around is soothing. Falling asleep in your presence is comforting on its own. If you keep going back to soothe then you are defeating the object.)

◆ If your puppy is chewing something he shouldn't that is not attached to you, don't tell him off – he is doing what comes naturally. He needs to chew to develop his 'chewing' muscles, to remove baby teeth and promote the eruption of his adult teeth. Instead, call him to you and give him something he is allowed to chew.

◆ If he does not come to you, quietly approach him – no eye contact or vocals – gently remove the object you don't want him to chew, and replace it with an acceptable object.

CHAPTER 12
Learning with Age-Appropriate Play

We play with them as puppies, so let's be fun and never stop playing into adulthood. Playing together creates a bond and is the best tool for learning.

Don't rough and tumble with him (this is what puppies do to one another; you are the adult). Yes (before you say it!), their parents *do* play rough and tumble with them, but they are canines and know how to get it right – with all the subtle body language. Unless you have ears and a tail, and can bark (or are very lucky), it is a perilously fine line to tread when you try to replicate canine games.

A prime example is tug of war – it's great for dogs, but humans nearly always get it wrong. Not only do they stress the puppy out by overexciting him, but they also place his neck in the very vulnerable position of looking upwards, which is unnatural and causes damage to one so young. With an older dog, the pressure on the spine to formed bones and joints is something like whiplash.

We have seen our mother dogs playing this game with their puppies, and it is a joy to watch. This game teaches them that sometimes they win and sometimes they lose, so in essence to judge when it is wise to stand and when to yield. Most importantly the parent dogs are always calm and controlled when they play with their puppies – they keep the excitement level within acceptable parameters at all times, and when the puppy becomes over the top, they pause the game until it winds down. Watch a mother with her child whether human or dog – they will keep it all calm.

Humans often do not have this sense with puppies; they think that the more excited the puppy becomes, the more fun it gets from the game, and will think it hilarious when their puppy fastens on to the end of a tug toy to swing him around by their teeth.

Some 'experts' tell us that the game is fine just so long as the dog is never allowed to win. But we believe that this game is best left to the canines, as when played with humans it can quickly get out of hand. Your dog could observe your determination to win and think that the 'game' has morphed into a battle of strength. He might decide to get the toy from you by going for your end of the rope and inadvertently (at *first*) nipping your hand, causing you to immediately drop the tug toy. But what has he learned now? A dog going for your end of the rope is the equivalent of two dogs going mouth to mouth – it rarely ends well.

Instead, here are some games you can play safely with your dog, where there are no winners or losers, just two creatures having fun. You will teach them some useful skills too.

Come Here: Recall Training Part 1

This simple game is the beginning of recall training. Do this as a matter of course whenever you want to interact with your puppy. Even if he is next to you and looking for interaction, simply step away and call him to you. This will help enormously to gain perfect recall when you really need it out and about.

Dogs do not call each other unless they are out of sight and need direction back or they just need an indication of where everyone is. If recall has not been established, repeated calling when you can't see your pup is saying to them, 'I'm over here, when you are ready' – you have turned the recall word into 'I'm here' not 'Come back'!

Puppies are naturally inquisitive, so simply scratching the ground with no eye contact will get your pup running over to you. Pop in your word for 'Come here', then praise him when he gets to you, and you have introduced the recall word in a natural, non-stressful way. If you don't want them to join you digging the garden (or similar), simply guide away with no recall word and no eye contact. Walk away if necessary and repeat to get the message across. This is natural canine communication at its simplest; it is exactly what they do to each other: either welcome, rebuff or ignore the presence of another.

Make an effort to always call your puppy to you for interaction. If everything he gets from you is on your terms, recall is established regardless of the situation

◆ Begin Come Here at home, from the word go. Decide what indicator you are going to use to ask your puppy to return to you. It could be verbal or non-verbal – both is best, and make yourself inviting.

◆ Scratch the ground, rustle leaves, etc., or use his name to get his attention.

◆ When he looks to you, or has already started to move towards you, say your recall word (for instance, 'Here') and crouch down with arms outstretched. Always follow the calling of his name with a clear indicator of what you require from him. The puppy's name isn't enough on its own – if someone called your name, your response would be along the lines of 'Yes, what do you want?'

◆ Continue with 'Good boy!' or other very encouraging sounds as he runs or potters towards you.

◆ As he gets close, draw your hands towards you. Doing this will draw your puppy close to you. Remember not to 'stare your puppy out' – prolonged and intense eye contact can make canines feel very uncomfortable. If your puppy is showing reluctance, and you suspect this is the case, turn sideways to your puppy and use only intermittent eye contact. This is less intimidating.

◆ Do not go for his head immediately as this will appearing threatening and make him back off. Your hands need to be clearly welcoming and kind. Similarly, do not grab him by the neck or collar, or lunge at him in any way. You draw him close by encouragement, and your welcoming body language.

- When he is well on his way to returning, move away in a crouched position, encouraging him with 'Good boy!' as he follows you. (This is also the beginnings of Follow Me.) Movement is a powerful tool, and dogs are driven by movement creating the chase.
- When your puppy gets to you, continue praise and gently stroke or massage. You can give him the occasional treat in the form of food, but do not lure him with the food – that is bribery not reward.
- Hold your puppy while massaging him, and when you are finished simply let go. By doing this you are the one that initiates contact and you also indicate that he is now free to go – your puppy will learn to respond to your call, and to learn patience when he has arrived – he cannot just dash off again immediately.
- If your puppy is engrossed with a bee or flower – or anything else for that matter – get close, in his eyeline, and call his name just once to get his attention. You may have to touch him gently to get him into your world.
- Then, when he shows his attention by turning to you, say the recall word and run back a few paces and crouch down. Praise as before when he comes.

You don't need any commands like sit and stay; they are unnecessary and take the fun out of fun – what meaning do sit and stay have for a puppy? His mother doesn't use them. Be proactive and have some imagination with everything you do. If he jumps up, place his paws down and then stroke and massage and praise.

Paws for Thought

If a puppy does not come when called when he has his nose down a mole hole, he isn't ignoring you. He is so absorbed in what he's found and all those delicious smells, he just doesn't hear you. Get close, get low, be fun – and make it happen kindly.

Follow Me

This game is the very beginning of lead work.

◆ Begin by attracting your puppy's attention, then call him into your space.

◆ Maintaining warm eye contact, bend over, with hands in front of your body and about one or two feet from the ground, and encourage your puppy to follow you. Keep your vocals happy and inviting.

◆ Continuously pat your hands together, swaying your arms from side to side, and your puppy will follow your patting hands.

◆ Start moving around the room or garden, encouraging him to follow you with your patting hands.

◆ Maintain eye contact throughout, but if your puppy shows discomfort by not joining in, then make the eye contact intermittent to take the pressure off.

◆ Be aware – keep the puppy thinking but not overreacting. Do stop every so often, and in any case keep the sessions short and fun.

◆ Do not let your puppy reach a reactionary state. However, if you missed the moment and he becomes 'wound up' (jumping, nipping and barking), stop engaging with your puppy – and this means no eye contact, too – until he calms down. Then invite him to join you for a gentle massage. Have another go later in the day.

Hide and Seek

This is a good one to play when your pup's attention is elsewhere.

◆ Hide behind a tree. Keep your puppy in view without him being able to see you.

◆ Call him, again without making yourself visible.

◆ When he finds you, give a big fun-filled welcome.

Fetch It (leading to) Find It

◆ Throw a toy, and your puppy will most likely run after it.

◆ When he's picked it up, call him and run in the other direction.

◆ Receive the toy side on, with lots of praise. This is Fetch It.

◆ Don't make constant eye contact, as this is when your pup can get in to the conversation of, 'You want this? I'm not bringing it back! I've got your attention – watch me and chase me.'

◆ When he's got the idea of bringing the toy back to you each time, you can progress to the game of Find It.

◆ Leave your puppy in a separate room so he can't see what's going on.

◆ Hide his toy or toys in the garden or another room.

◆ Let him in the space, and help him Find It by directing with your arm.

◆ If he's struggling, help him. Go closer to the toy.

◆ If he's still confused, give the toy movement by shoving it with your hand or foot.

◆ When he has picked it up, take some steps back and encourage him to bring it to you.

Don't Chase It

This is a good game to teach when your puppy is settled in and loves finding balls you have hidden – at about four to five months old. Learning not to chase something can help prevent ball obsession and animal chasing later.

◆ Start in your house and garden. Drop a toy just to your side, the opposite side from your puppy, preferably in long grass or bush (outside) or a piece of furniture (inside) so that he doesn't have a visual trigger.

◆ Encourage your pup to follow you. Walk backwards so you are facing him – this is the best and easiest way for your puppy to fully engage with you on this one.

◆ As he does, give constant praise, then, when you are ready, go find the ball with him.

◆ As he gets better at this, which will take a few weeks, you can drop the ball and leave it in view, down by your side, and encourage your puppy to walk on with you. By teaching him this, neither a still ball nor a moving ball will flick his 'chase' drive, as it's all about you.

◆ Swap the ball for other items, such as children's toys and clothing and remote controls, to walk away from. These items are not theirs, and to be shown this way is far less stressful than a 'leave it' command. Then you can go find a toy or ball they can fetch for you.

◆ In time, as you move forwards and see animals he may want to chase, all you have to do is turn and back away and praise him as he follows you.

◆ By not letting your dog pull after anything, and instead turning and encouraging him to refocus on you each time, the drive to chase will have been diverted to contact with you.

◆ You can give a food reward when he does this or, better still, Find It with ball or toy you have hidden previously, or Fetch It with something you want him to chase and bring back – chase this but not that!

◆ (We will move on to this in Chapter 15, but please, when out and about, have your puppy on a long lead and harness. He *will* want to chase squirrels, rabbits and sheep, etc. A long lead and harness will stop him getting it wrong with no way of you being able to guide him right. If your dog is chasing or worrying any farm animal, the farmer is quite within his rights to shoot him.

Be inventive with play. Don't repeatedly throw a ball and expect your dog to come back with it. Your puppy will either get bored and stop playing altogether or get completely obsessed with this exercise, which really isn't healthy for the growing body or mind.

It's important when you begin to ensure there is no pressure on them to perform in any of these games – pressure gives rise to confusion, stress and failure. Our expectations have to be age appropriate and land within their capabilities. (See Julia Robertson's book and DVD in Resources for more information.)

Paws for Thought: Food Rewards

Keep these few and far between, or you'll get a puppy that will only perform for food. The reward has got to be about you, not what you possess.

Agility

You can try low-key agility, but with no jumping before eighteen months of age. Trotting over and around stepping poles (these are like agility jumping poles but laid on the ground) will be fun for you and your puppy, and have the added benefit of, again, educating him to follow you. You are having fun and the pup will want to be with you. This is the beginnings of heel work.

One Paw at a Time: Learning to Walk on a Lead with Follow Me

We are in no rush to get puppies on a lead. It is an action that needs great trust and understanding. When dogs walk together in a natural environment, they are quite widely spread – but they always keep an eye out for each other and especially for the one who is the ultimate decision maker. They know that if they get separated from the family they could get into difficulties on their own.

With this in mind, when you start teaching walking on the lead in the garden, and then out in the park, have your pup on a longer 'training lead' (two to three metres) and play Come Here and Follow Me – with intermittent sniffy time so the lesson is not too intense and they have time to be themselves and investigate their surroundings. Lead work and recall go hand in hand. If you have no connection (apart from the physical) with your dog when he is on the lead, you will not have his focus when you let him off.

◆ You will have already started Follow Me off lead in your house and garden (page 86). There is no time limit to getting it right. Be patient.

◆ Then move to attaching a lead. Do not hold it but leave it dragging, as tension on the lead at this stage will stress him out or get him into a game of tug.

◆ Ideally, the lead needs to be about two to three metres long and attached to a soft harness.

◆ Pick it up now and again with no pressure.

◆ Your pup will only tug or chew at the lead if the lesson is too early in his life, you are creating too much pressure to learn, or if he is tired: in which case end your training session for now – remove the lead, stop the game, call him to you and praise him for that. Lead work needs to be done slowly but surely.

◆ Do not change and become the 'heel demon' by using either bribery or coercion. You are encouraging your pup to be with you, but not forcing a close association at a time when all he really wants to do is investigate.

◆ If you find your puppy is more interested in the lead than you, then the desired connection has not truly established. There is nothing to gain and everything to lose by buying into the game of 'tug' – go back to off-lead Follow Me, and progress at a slower pace. There is no rush.

◆ When he accepts the three-metre lead, build up by holding it more frequently and for longer periods.

◆ Walk backwards initially, have a toy with you, make yourself interesting. Continue to look to your puppy, so when he glances up he is immediately rewarded with your kind and happy face.

◆ If he jumps up, stop, pop his paws down, no eye contact, no speech. When he is calm again, continue.

◆ As always, keep lessons short and sweet. If he loses focus, call him back, have another go. It's not his fault, and he may feel stressed and need a break. Finish on a good note.

◆ If he goes in front to the point that he is pulling you forwards, stop and rest. Then walk backwards to gain eye contact. Reward and praise when he is with you.

◆ Still within home boundary, practise at least four times a day, increase the time gradually as you and he get better. Go at his learning speed.

When he is walking with you, give eye contact, and reward and praise regularly.

Testing Your Puppy's Focus on You

The stop is as important as walking.

◆ Stop every now and again – if your pup is focused on you, he will stop, too. Praise him.

◆ If, however, he carries on, let him – he will stop when he gets to the end of the lead. Call him to you and begin again.

◆ Try just moving one foot forward and stop. This shows him that just because you've done A, it doesn't mean B is going to happen. This will focus your pup on you and stop him trying to pre-empt your next move.

Moving On To a Shorter Lead for Street Walking

◆ Progress to walking your puppy on a shorter lead, in preparation for street walking.

◆ Zig zag about and be fun.

◆ Be relaxed at every stage.

◆ If you lose your pup's focus, go back to where you had it and begin again. Try once more, then stop the exercise.

Tricks

If you'd like to teach lie down, give a paw, roll over, etc., do it in a fun way, but don't teach sit before he is twelve to eighteen months, when the growing plates have fixed. Before then, just let your puppy sit naturally or lie down when he wants to. Remember, none of our requests are a natural instruction from canine to canine, so keep training short and sweet and don't bribe. There is no rush. It is better to enjoy the time spent learning just how to be together with your new friend, without trying to make him perform these strange human tricks.

All things come to those who are patient and work at it in a level-headed fun manner. It will all happen – and remember there is no time limit. Don't skip to adulthood and miss out on childhood. And when you get to adulthood, don't forget to keep the fun going or your relationship will stagnate.

Some people think certain breeds won't ever play, or come back, or heel. Given the right attitude and teacher, every puppy has the potential to do it all. If you start off being a defeatist, then you reap what you sow. Likewise, all breeds can exhibit all behavioural problems known to man. Don't pigeonhole your pup because of breed. If you've chosen a puppy from a good home and give it the right advice, then you'll breeze through. If you've chosen a rescue pup, with a dubious start in life, you may find you've brought trouble home – it's not necessarily going to be straightforward, but it will be very rewarding indeed.

CHAPTER 13

Teaching More Than One Puppy

Treat them as Individuals

The most important thing to remember about teaching two puppies is to treat them as individuals. They need to learn to love and respect you as the decision maker, not to rely on each other. Each will have different personalities and learning abilities – don't expect them to learn at the same pace; they will 'get it' in their own time. As with any educational programme, you must listen and watch your pupils.

By having individual time you will also be preventing separation anxiety between them. There will be times when one has to go to the vet, and you don't want either to be stressed out during this forced separation.

We want each pup to learn that he is important in his own right, and that he can come for a cuddle or groom without the other pushing it out of the way. Don't always call your pups at the same time. You'll find when you call one pup over that they both come. This is normal, but something which they must learn is not acceptable. Sometimes you may make an all-encompassing invitation – meaning that all are welcome – but the puppies must gradually learn to differentiate between the two.

By guiding the interloper to the side very gently (not holding skin or fur) and saying nothing, he will learn to respect the other's space and your space, and above all patience. Don't feel cruel, just remember – when you ask one of your human family members to sit on your lap, you don't expect to be crushed by everyone taking the liberty of doing the same! They will all get a piece of you when you decide. Special one-to-one time is important for each and every one of us, including our dogs; it's not a case of anyone missing out.

Food

Feed them at the same time in the same room, but stand between them so, if one finishes first, or decides he wants what the other has, then you can intercept buy moving the pup away back to his bowl. Not a word should be spoken when putting the puppy right.

It's good to give them chews – give them safe stag antlers under supervision. When one attempts to steal the other's, your response is the same as with their meals. And the same with toys! If one is pushing the other out the way because 'I want what he's got!' – don't let them bully but do let them play.

Puppy Play

You will need to play some team games separately to start with – place one behind a baby gate or a screen they can view from. When they are playing together, ensure one does not always get the toy by gently holding one dog back while you go hunt for the toy with the other. When the puppy that has been allowed to get the toy returns with it for you, ensure the one you have held off is kept to the side of you, so the other can come close with confidence in the knowledge that he is not going to be mugged.

We always suggest a game of Find It (page 87), as it uses their natural abilities and hones their noses, and makes them think more rather than react (as in a game of throw and fetch). It also is a far gentler game to play, and therefore doesn't put unnecessary strain on immature bones and ligaments. On top of this it teaches the puppy to be a team player with you.

It is great for them to play together, but if you feel play is getting too over the top, step in and calm it all down. Walk between them and they should move apart. If this doesn't work, you may have to gently guide them apart – without a word (or this raucous play will become an attention-seeking behaviour), place your hands gently on their sides and show them how to be calm by being calm yourself.

Follow Me

When you get to lead work, you must do it individually, just as with the game of Follow Me off lead. The first steps for on-lead work are found in Chapter 12, on pages 89–91. Then Chapter 15 takes us out into the wider world.

When each puppy is happily managing walks outside the house separately, the next step is to take both pups out together. Put one each side of you and move out slowly from home, as you did on an individual basis. They will try to push their luck and pull in front or play and certainly not be as good as they were on their own. Just repeat the exercise, as you would with individual work, and they will settle day by day as you practise. Again, keep these lessons short, as it's all new and exciting and another little stressful learning curve.

Your puppies will have different levels of learning and attention. Be patient; one will respond to different areas better than the other, but they will catch up with each other in the end.

CHAPTER 14

Vets, Vaccines and Neutering

If your puppy reacts to pain by growling and yelping or nipping, this is not aggression, it is an intrinsic defence mechanism! If you have followed the instructions in Chapter 5, you will have made sure that your pup was used to being gently handled by the breeder, and he will be relaxed and happy to be massaged and held by you and your family members. His next significant handler is the vet.

Make your pup's first vet experience a good one. Visit the vets just for a check-up and 'getting to know you' session soon after arrival, and then wait for a few days or a week before his first vaccine.

It is often best to find out about recommended vets by word of mouth. But even if someone comes recommended, be vigilant when you visit – as ever, do not allow anyone to push their faces into your puppy's face or use other behaviour that will be overbearing for your pup.

One Paw at a Time: A First Vet Visit

◆ When you first visit the vet, don't go only because your puppy is due for treatment. Go there for your puppy to experience a 'call over' and a massage from the vet or veterinary nurse.

◆ To help your puppy accept it with confidence, stand next to the person, showing the puppy you are happy in this stranger's space.

◆ Do not let them loom over the puppy or stare him in the eye, even if they're saying, 'Lovely puppy'.

◆ Instead, ask them to kneel down and call your puppy to them, with intermittent or, better still, no eye contact.

◆ If you follow these instructions, your puppy will learn that when he goes to the vet he gets lovely things.

Teaching Restraint

Puppies have to be shown that touch and restraint are not bad things. When stroking, or better still massaging, your puppy, always do it gently. By massaging him all over from the start, he gets used to being handled. Don't lunge for a stroke, placing your hands over his eyes. By always calling your puppy over to you, he will feel safe and nurtured rather than attacked.

Show the puppy that restraint is only going to reap good things. Restrain him for short periods with a gentle hold, and release before he shows tension. Start with just a few seconds, and build up gradually to longer sessions – this will give your puppy confidence in you, and those who you trust, to do the same.

Paws for Thought

Vaccinations

When it comes to vaccines and boosters, there has been – and will continue to be – a bewildering wealth of conflicting advice. Make up your own minds. We have included some useful website links in the Resources at the back of this book.

Castration and Spaying

It should be a matter of common sense that it is not a good idea to spay or neuter your puppy before it is fully mature. You'll be taking away their growth hormones so they can't mature into healthy adults, but despite this, puppies are routinely desexed well before their first birthday.

Many vets will tell you that there is absolutely nothing wrong with this, but I ask you – unless there is a life or death medical reason, would you ever consider that a child would not suffer huge trauma, and lifelong emotional and physical problems, if the same criteria were to be applied to humans? For dogs, many of the common physical and emotional issues are both well known and well documented.

Depending on the size of the breed, dogs reach maturity at different ages; do not castrate or spay until completely mature. Even then, consider the option of less radical surgery – some vets are beginning to favour giving males a vasectomy and females a partial spay leaving ovaries intact. This keeps both sexes mentally and physically fit and helps prevent many cancers and illnesses.

However, we appreciate that you will not be given a choice if you take a puppy/adolescent dog from a rescue centre, and we do understand why they have this policy. It is impossible to implement the ideal solution when these centres are inundated on a daily basis with abused or unwanted dogs – they cannot in all conscience allow dogs to leave their care able to produce six to eight more unwanted puppies within nine weeks.

Sometimes vets will recommend castration in order to reduce behavioural issues. In our opinion, castration very rarely does this (except in the case of a dog who has an above-average testosterone level as an adult). Adolescents have a massive testosterone surge, but this levels out to normal when they mature. Neutering almost always exacerbates aggression rather than lessens it.

If you are concerned that castration or spaying will have a negative effect on your mature dog then ask your vet to do a chemical castration first. This is an implant which replicates surgical castration but wears off within a year; if it does have a negative emotional effect then you can elect not to surgically castrate. Once the tackle's gone, you can't sew it back on!

If you do not neuter, you will have to be vigilant and responsible when it comes to bitches in season. Whichever sex you have, you will need to keep your dog from roaming. There are so many unwanted dogs in rescues – don't let your dog contribute to them. Supervision and responsible dog ownership is paramount.

We have listed a useful website that outlines recent neutering research in the Resources section. Why, how and when you neuter your dog is ultimately up to you – but please do your homework.

CHAPTER 15

The World Beyond your Front Door

Your puppy is twelve to sixteen weeks and all vaccinated – so ready for the outside world as far as protection from disease is concerned. You have been playing Follow Me on the long lead at home and progressed to a shorter lead in preparation for walking on the street. But how prepared is he to be bombarded with all the new sights and sounds around him beyond your garden and home? Quite honestly, he's not equipped to face all these new experiences. He will need someone to look to for guidance and protection, someone who has oodles of patience and understanding – *you*.

It is said that, in order for him to become a well-socialised and acceptable adult dog, we need to introduce a puppy to all he is going to be faced with throughout his life before he is sixteen weeks of age (some advise fourteen weeks).

For us, that's like taking a toddler to a theme park, a sweet shop, a disco and then dropping them out of a plane on a parachute – then expecting him to remain of sound mind. Would he have a good night's sleep or want to go again?

We know that acquainting a puppy to everything so quickly will freak him out. He would either become quiet and withdrawn or so fearful that he would start lashing out at things, places, people or dogs – or you – in order to keep his space safe. The knock-on effect is that he loses faith in you, and your ability to keep him safe, wondering what you are going to lead him into next.

With this in mind, introduce your puppy to each aspect of the out-side world in his own time. Keep an eye on his body language and walk him away as necessary. In this chapter, we take you step by step through this important process.

Paws for Thought

Dogs don't do cowardice or bravery. They do whatever it takes to be safe, whether that means running or fighting.

As we know, puppies learn best through play and with a light-hearted teacher. Also, we all feel safer and happier with boundaries and guidelines. The greatest gift you can give to your child or puppy (or friend or relative) is the knowledge that you make great choices – you make the right decisions when you need you to and at the right time. They are safe with you, you are their rock, you understand them, you are their everything.

Dogs and children need this more than adults. Adults need it when they lose their way or just need someone to help them make a good decision. But with a dog – puppy or adult – you need to be the trusted one that they turn to.

With all this in mind, you have to make choices for your young charge. You decide who to be with and who to play with, and where is the best place to learn life skills.

One Paw at a Time: Introducing Puppy to the Street

◆ As an initial introduction, sit quietly in the front garden, with your puppy at your side. Just watch the world and its noisy occupants go by. Your puppy can take in the sights and sounds at a safe distance, within a safe environment, and with his calm, confident and quiet protector at his side. If your home has no front garden but your front door opens straight onto the street, you can still sit on the front doorstep with your puppy behind you – he can take in the sights and sounds from his position of being behind a secure buffer (that's you!).

◆ If he reacts to vehicles in a fearful way, take him back indoors quietly, without fuss or coddling.

◆ The next time you are ready to enter the front garden, start Follow Me (page 86) on the lead in the house and seamlessly progress to the front garden.

◆ When he is happy with this, go for a few yards up the road in a game of Follow Me on your short lead – or a little further if he seems happy – then return towards home. Ideally, you will return home before anything causes him to feel uncomfortable, making a stress-free and enjoyable first outing. If an approaching vehicle – or anything else – does cause him alarm, simply turn away from the vehicle and return home without fuss.

◆ If you do not have a front garden, you will need to move from the watching to going-out phase very gradually. As ever, be very aware of your puppy's body language and be ready to turn away from any cause of discomfort and return home without fuss.

◆ Continue to be as inventive and inspiring as you were on home ground, keeping a 50-metre radius initially. Even in such a small area you can vary your route. Leave the house by either turning left or right, and crossing the road at any point when it is safe. Keep your puppy thinking about you and where you are going.

◆ You can even drive to a different location to increase the number of sights and sounds. In these cases, use your car as home base.

◆ Turning away from your puppy's fear and returning home (or to 'home base') will in time result in your pup getting solace from just turning and walking away from the fear or uncertainty.

◆ Increase the length and location of his outings bit by bit, as he gains confidence in you. Always keep your body as a buffer between your puppy and the things which cause him fear.

◆ If your puppy has already become fearful and confrontational with all (or some) of the sights and sounds of the greater world, the process of desensitisation is exactly the same as for the initial points above. As with any unacceptable activities, it takes time and patience to reverse a fear behaviour, but by persevering you will be successful.

One Paw at a Time: Acclimatising to the World Outside

◆ Movement is a powerful tool. Get your puppy focused on you and keep him moving, then he will see you are unfazed and accept a situation.

◆ Sniffy time is very important, so he can find out about his world. Stop on your walk and let him do what comes naturally.

◆ You can use Come Here to reinforce recall when he is engrossed in all these lovelies. You need recall as your fail-safe, so make sure it works when your puppy is minding its own business. (See pages 105–6 below for more on recall.) Getting him back into your world at a touch of a button is the most important safety tactic there is.

◆ People can stroke him when you are out and about *if* he is calm, and *if* they call him to them and he responds by moving towards them. Always watch his body language.

◆ If he is reluctant to approach the person, you can try standing next to them and engaging with this person yourself. He may well decide to approach a little later when he feels more confident. If he is still uncomfortable, put yourself between the puppy and the person, and if that doesn't help, simply say goodbye and walk away.

◆ If you have your puppy on a longer (always loose) line in a safe park area, he has the opportunity to find out about his world in a relaxed manner and you will be able to put him right and help him as needed.

◆ Be in tune with your puppy's silent communication signals. (See the Brenda Aloff and Turid Rugaas books in the Resources for more details.)

Paws for Thought: The Best Teacher

The best teacher for your pre-school child is you. The best teacher for your puppy is you. Popular people are the ones who are kind and considerate and make good decisions. We want your puppy to love, like and trust you, so never put yourself out there as anything but that person. Patience and consistency is a must. If you're not getting the right response from your puppy or your friend or your child, don't blame them: look to change yourself. If you change you, everyone changes around you – for good or bad.

People follow those who show all the best attributes, as do animals. Be a teacher, not a trainer. You are there to guide your puppy through things he doesn't understand. If he shows fear, walk away together, using an encouraging voice – he then does not have to endure the experience and will look to you with admiration and trust. The next time you come across the same object or being, you do the same, until the puppy trusts you to pass it by.

One Paw at a Time: Patience While Out and About on a Lead

Your puppy can learn to walk and stop with you naturally. There is no need to ask him to sit, he will do it anyway if you stop for any length of time. If you bug him to sit, sit and sit, then you become tense and upset and your puppy agitated and confused. Instead:

◆ When you stop, praise your puppy for stopping.

◆ If he wiggles and tugs on the lead when you have your attention else-where, simply call him back and praise him when he's by your side.

◆ Stroke and touch your puppy, so he feels you with him, but do not speak.

◆ If you're having a conversation, he may try to jump up and get your eye contact. Gently guide him down with no speech or eye contact and then have physical contact only – speaking will only enforce that he can get your attention.

◆ Don't stay to chat too long. There is only so long a puppy can say still.

◆ Repeat regularly, so it becomes the norm.

◆ As he gets older, the length of time you stop can increase. In time he will naturally wait and most probably will lie down by you.

One Paw at a Time: Recall Training Part 2 and Other Long Lead Work

◆ In the park, attach a long line of about nine metres to your puppy's harness.

◆ If he doesn't come when called, you can take hold of the line (but don't pull) and, when he looks to you, say your recall word and run back a few paces and crouch down.

◆ Praise as before when he comes.

◆ Puppies and dogs get absorbed in everything around them. Usually, it is not that your puppy is deliberately ignoring you, he just doesn't hear you. So, as with in your garden, you can use touch to bring him back to your world – the touch in this case comes down the line.

◆ There will be things he wants to investigate, so let him have his sniffy time too. People get lead work wrong because they make their puppy work too hard. Puppies need to investigate, but we must have a way to redirect them so they do not get so absorbed in their own world and log off you completely.

- Also play Follow Me. Walking with you does not mean his head glued by your knee, with his neck straining to catch your eye contact. If this *is* needed for activities in adulthood, teach it in adulthood. It is too much pressure for a puppy.
- Remember to add variety. Play Find It, trotting over sticks or poles, and Hide and Seek. Be inventive.
- You will progress day by day, and week by week. There is no rush, just enjoy the process.
- Initially when you change direction, use a simple recall if he is otherwise distracted. In time, your dog will be so tuned into you that you will always be in his mind and he will keep an eye on where you are going, rather than the other way round. You can relax in the knowledge that he wants to be with you and follow you as you are fun, loving and trustworthy.

Be consistent, and take these gradual steps, and your puppy will learn to recall consistently, and will develop into the dog who comes *always* when asked.

When you are confident of your pups recall and connection to you on a long line, now is the time to set him free. There is no timescale to this, but do be aware just because he is great at sixteen weeks the lesson is not fully learnt. He will go through many more testing and learning phases up to adulthood. Always be prepared to take a step back and readdress any lesson. Even then, just because he's an adult it is in a dog's nature to constantly question your credentials as a decision maker. Never become complacent; it is an ongoing project.

Paws for Thought: Heel?

Walking with you and following you is natural; 'heel' on a lead is not. There is no reason for hard and fast rules, such as 'the head has to be one inch to the left of your left knee and not more than one inch in front of your knee'. If your puppy stops and starts with you, that's great, but lighten up and enjoy it. When dogs walk together, it is never at heel.

One Paw at a Time: Longer Walks

Long walks are not physically great for puppies – puppy free play together is the best thing for learning to be a dog and exercising appropriately (see overleaf). But when your puppy is about four months old you can introduce some longer walks.

◆ At four months, your puppy will be ready for two 15-minute walks a day. Build in a close destination for play.
◆ At six months, you can try two 30-minute walks. Again, build in some play.
◆ Don't be predictable – don't go the same way every time.
◆ Be relaxed at every stage. If you lose your pup's focus, go back to where you had it and begin again.
◆ Be prepared to call off the destination you were wanting to get to. You'll get there one day, but your object is for your puppy to learn, not to go from A to B.

Paws for Thought

Do not rely on the lead: it is not a form of correction, only a connection. If you tug and pull, your pup will get stressed and push against it. Remember, it is your inviting body language that encourages your puppy to walk with you. If that is wrong, you will not achieve your goal.

Playing with their Peers and Older Dogs

At the same time as you are playing Recall and Follow Me with your puppy in the park, you can start introducing him to other dogs. It's important to get this right from the off.

Choose his friends wisely. Choose puppies of a similar size, personality and age, and let them play in an open garden or other safe space, where they can get to know each other in the way they do naturally, and in their own time

When encountering adult dogs, ideally make sure you know the other dog and owner. And set the ground rules. (See Chapter 10, for more on your puppy meeting and playing with older dogs.)

Puppy free play

Find out about puppy free-play sessions in your area. Choose a low-key class with a big space and no more than six puppies, all the same age and roughly the same size. Outside meeting places are great – the puppies have room to hide, play and interact without getting stressed by being too confined.

If there are none in your area, then find pups of a similar age and do it at home. Let pups be pups. Do not jump in and stop the rough and tumble. Pups before sixteen weeks are finding out how to interact with each other. They may make a dreadful noise, but generally it is just kiddy play. If you are concerned, then simply part the pups, without fuss, and hold them to calm them down before letting them continue to play and learn.

Paws for Thought

Humans see value in conquering our irrational fears because we know they are irrational and cannot hurt us. When dogs fear, their natural reaction is to avoid; they see no value in

---

confrontation. When dogs find themselves in a stressful situation, they do not think, they react, so to force them to 'face their fear' will cause them stress, and will not achieve a positive result.

Meeting dogs on the lead

Start with a dog and owner you already know, in a low-stimulus location – you know the quiet times and places in your own area. Once your puppy or adolescent has learned self-control, then meetings on lead will be gentle and stress-free with your guidance.

Potential meetings off lead

When off lead, don't let your young dog bound over to an unknown dog – you don't know what that dog's reaction is going to be. It is the same with humans – many humans have a huge fear of dogs, even little ones and puppies – and it is not fair to let your puppy run up to them. You may love your puppy or baby, but not everyone wants sticky fingers, or snot, or paw prints, all over their clothing. People or dogs who quite rightly want to mind their own business, and do not want an exuberant youngster or bully in their midst, get angry and upset. Be a responsible dog owner and have empathy for everyone else out there. Walk with your puppy to and fro towards a friend until your puppy walks beside you and arrives at your friend with you, not dragging you. And keep your puppy on a long line until you know you have great recall.

Paws for Thought

Be a wise owner and observe the body language of approaching dogs. It is too late when your dog (or you) has been attacked.

Take responsibility for yourself and your dog to avoid potential trouble. Do this and you will never have to hear 'Oh he's never done that before' when you or your dog has been intimidated by a growling dog – or worse, been on the receiving end of a bite. You can bet your bottom dollar that either the owner has missed the signals leading up to the reaction, or their dog has done it before.

CHAPTER 16

How your Behaviour Affects your Puppy

How you are, your behaviour and frame of mind when correcting or 'explaining' what you require from your puppy, will always affect *his* behaviour, and his desire and ability to learn – either in a positive or negative way.

If you are an enthusiastic, friendly, but also a calm and well-balanced teacher; if you are prepared to show him (patiently and without any sign of bad temper or frustration) what you want from him – as many times as is necessary; if you discourage unacceptable behaviour by giving him nothing but appropriate redirection; if you react to every compliance with your requests in a praise-filled and encouraging way – in short, if you are a good parent and teacher, your puppy will happily become an attentive and willing pupil.

If you are calm, well-balanced, patient and friendly, your attitude will become your puppy's attitude. He will absorb your unflustered, gentle but confident mindset, and reflect it in his own behaviour. Unfortunately, if you are impatient, aggressive, unjust and randomly inconsistent, and you punish for 'wrong' behaviour, never showing what you *do* want, you will find that you have created a dog with either aggressive, nervous or generally manic behaviour.

The choice is yours.

Paws for Thought

Never send your dog away for training (unless sometimes for training in assistance work). You don't know what they do when you are not around, and you need your dog to respond only to you and to work with you, not anyone else.

So many humans are very quick to 'tell off' their puppy when he has done something they do not like, without showing him in a calm and controlled way what it is that they *do want*. Conversely, when he has behaved in an acceptable way (doing something just as they would like it done) they take the attitude, 'Well about blooming time too!' and do not give the praise he is due – the praise which would have told him that his actions pleased his human, and that this is how he should respond in future to this situation.

A good example is recall.

How many times have you heard an owner bellowing 'Charlieeeeee!!', in increasingly loud and angry tones to his dog? This sergeant-major voice – would you find it inviting? Already the owner has created an unfriendly atmosphere.

He continues to bellow. The dog knows exactly where his owner is, so does not feel lost and alone. He also knows from past experience that however quickly he comes now, he is going to get a hostile reception – so he puts off the evil moment for as long as possible. (In the worst case, depending upon the level of 'reprisal' he has received in the past and upon his personality, he just disappears into the wide blue yonder.)

When (or if) he does return, she uses canine calming signals to try to take the heat out of the situation. He will walk very slowly, often curving away to sniff at something. He will lick his lips, he may stop walking and gaze away into the distance.

All of these actions are what canines do if they are approaching an unfriendly canine – or if they are simply not sure of their reception. They are designed to show the other dog that they are friendly, they are not disrespectfully charging into their space, they are giving the other dog time to take them in and realise that they pose no threat – they are also creating time for them to slowly walk away themselves if they do not want to interact.

These actions are instinctive, performed naturally in an attempt to calm the angry human.

But what happens?

The human, already with steam coming out of his ears, completely misreads the signs. He thinks the dog is walking so slowly, and doing all the other things, either because 'he knows he is naughty', or because he is deliberately taking his time to tick his owner off.

So, after all her efforts to calm the situation, the poor dog gets the telling off of her life *after* he has actually complied with the request – however late in coming. He has been punished for doing as his owner asked.

Instead, the good owner will keep things calm and encouraging from the dog's earliest days.

Your puppy is not deaf. He may well be so absorbed in sniffing and investigating that, on the first call, your voice has either not impinged on his consciousness, or has only floated on the very periphery of it.

Stop calling after the first couple of attempts, stand still and wait, and eventually your puppy will look up to see where you are. At this point you can call again in an enthusiastic and inviting way – running backwards, clapping your hands, anything to make yourself more interesting and compelling than whatever it is that stopped your puppy recalling instantly. If he looks up but goes back to what he was doing, then you wait again and repeat.

Eventually your puppy *will* return. Swallow your frustration and praise him to the skies!

If you do this when he is learning, he will realise that to come quickly is to receive all the praise in the world, from the human to whom he is becoming increasingly bonded and wants to be beside. To ignore your call becomes unacceptable to *him*, as he is learning, from this (and from every other area of his education), to do everything to please you, because he *wants* to – not because he *has* to.

Once this desirable behaviour is learned as a puppy, you will never have the need for the 'Charlieeeeee!!' scenario – your dog will recall to you as second nature.

Pressure to perform is massive for a puppy, pressure for the sit, heel, come here and of course 'don't do that'. Those who deliver these kind of commands in a pressurised way will not get the result they wish; they will receive the response they made.

Paws for Thought

It's Not About Breed

Whatever breed you have, all puppies can all learn to walk well on a lead, come back when called, play retrieving and finding games, and above all be relaxed and happy wherever you are. They can all learn if you teach with patience and praise.

How you interact with your dog will affect how your dog understands you, or not. How you feed, play, re-join, give affection and deal with uncertainties all have a bearing on how he connects to you. Teach your dog the way he learns and there will be understanding and a connection, a bond of trust and love that never fails.

Dogs learn from the minute they are born, as do we. They never stop learning, they never stop questioning or trying to understand. Recognise those uncertainties and answer them appropriately and your dog will be an extension of you.

Above all, have patience and take each day slowly, and don't try to make your new puppy run before he can walk. Do not pressure him to deal with experiences without you knowing what you need to do to make him feel secure.

Paws for Thought

It's what you *do*, not what you *say* that gets your puppy to respond to you in a positive way. If you are not getting the desired response for saying 'Here,' for example, stop and look at what you are doing. Are you side-on? Are you crouched down? Are you giving too much eye contact? Remember that you behaviour can cause him to switch off from you.

CHAPTER 17

Preventing Common Dog Problems

Almost all dog problems owners encounter stem from misunderstanding leading to stress for the dog. Stress manifests itself in unacceptable behaviours. All the preventative measures we outline in this chapter are equally applicable where problems already exist. So what causes stress?

Stress

The reasons for stress in dogs are many and various, but when living in a human environment the majority of stress-related behaviours are as a direct result of dogs a) trying to understand and cope with an unnatural way of living and b) being expected to recognise and comply with commands for unnatural behaviours without an essential bond of trust being established with their human.

If a dog has a kind and knowledgeable owner, most potentially stressful situations can either be avoided or made acceptable for our eminently adaptable dogs.

Almost all of the traditional training goals – sit, stay, heel, lie down, do not touch this food until I say (even though I have walked away, the canine signal that it is the next dog's turn to eat), etc. – are both meaningless and pointless to the canine mind. They are the human concept of a well-behaved dog; but a dog follows the 'rules' of cooperation and survival in a pack, and these human commands do not serve that goal at all.

However, although recall, staying close to our side when asked, not killing next door's cat or learning to walk with us while attached may not be natural to a canine mind, they are essential in our crowded, dangerous human world. They must become second nature for our domestic dogs. But is it necessary for your young puppy to perform these tasks all at once, in a robotic way, on stern command or in an enclosed hall (where there is no easy exit for those that find it too much), surrounded by other juveniles who just want to play and say 'hi'? Trying to learn in a stressful environment will have a negative effect that will stay with your pup for a lifetime.

Ask yourself, are you requiring a sit, lie down, etc., for the benefit of your dog – or to impress other humans with your control over him?

If you take the time to earn your puppy's trust, to patiently and gently introduce him to the mysteries of our world, and to show him that you are capable of guiding him and keeping him safe in that world, our more unnatural requests will be far more easy for him to accept – and without undue stress – at a time appropriate to age, which is when he is physically mature.

Make haste slowly, observe, and learn to understand your puppy. After all, this is what you expect from him – is it reasonable to expect less from yourself?

Learning any new life skill involves a degree of stress for all of us. If you introduce more advanced requests from a base of empathy and trust, the stress reduces to a level which is acceptable, and learning is possible.

Here is a recap of some key points to avoid stress:

◆ When you call him, treat him gently. Do not rev him up to a frenzy, as he will bite and mouth and 'stress out'.

◆ When he jumps up, don't say 'Down!' Show him what you want by placing his paws back on the ground and stroking him when he is back on four paws.

◆ Don't make him sit before a meal. As long as he is standing quietly, he gets his food.

◆ Don't stare at him when he eats, you are indicating you want it back and he may well not eat. Simply put food down and turn away, but remain in the room.

◆ Don't stare at him to constant check if he is going to go to sleep – he won't be able to! Could you?

◆ When you get up from a chair, don't look at him, as by doing so you are asking him to join you. Let him sleep, let him relax, and he will not become overly needy, and you will not be seen as needy either.

◆ When you want him to walk with you, play Follow Me off lead. Give no pressure, but be fun, then progress at a pace appropriate to his age (see Chapter 12).

◆ Play needs to be kind and gentle, without stress. Bombing around with you is mindless and accidents will happen.

◆ When anyone enters the house, let the puppy sniff them, find out about them in his own time and potter off. Then and only then can the newcomer step back and call for affection.

◆ If you are stressed he will be stressed.

◆ If you are calm and patient, your attitude to life will become your puppy's attitude to life.

Obsessive Behaviours

Obsessions are of our own making. They are an indication of a stressed or an out-of-control dog, and this is when accidents happen. Their adrenaline is sky high and it's not a good place to be, they are reactionary and non-thinking.

Obsessions often start in puppyhood, and usually for innocent or well-intentioned reasons. Play 'gone wrong' is a major cause of the most common obsessions. In our experience these are: ball obsession, chasing shadows or lights (particularly on walls within the home), frantic barking or chasing the vacuum cleaner, and adverse reactions to cars and motor bikes driving past in the street.

Ball obsessions

Ball obsession can start for the most well intentioned of reasons – that of interacting with your dog. The problems arise when play of this kind is not controlled by the human.

Most dogs enjoy chasing after a ball – it is the closest they get to chasing prey and 'bringing home the bacon'. However, things start to go pear-shaped when the game is demanded by the dog rather than instigated by the human.

If, from the outset, you decide when the game begins and when it ends, problems rarely arise – and you can do this by keeping the ball in a drawer when at home, producing it when you want the game to begin, and returning it to the drawer when you decide that it is to end. Similarly, when on a walk, produce the ball from your pocket, then return it when you have decided that the ball part of the walk has ended, or that an interval for your dog to engage in other activities is due.

If you are consistent with the 'rules', your dog will not question your right to control the times of play, and will recognise the termination procedure, accept that the game has ended and go off to do something else without fuss.

However, if you obsessively play ball, your dog will end up with ball obsession and rapidly drive you and him crazy!

A ball-obsessed dog wants you to throw the ball for him all the time – to the point of exhaustion for both of you. This can take many forms. He may constantly bring the ball to you, push it into your lap if you are sitting, nudge it towards you if you are standing or simply wander around with it in his mouth, constantly seeking eye contact with you to make you play.

This alone is irritating, but when he ups the ante to include bouncing and frantic barking at you, it can become intolerable.

When on a walk, a ball-obsessed dog will not be enjoying the normal canine pursuits of sniffing, investigating, meeting and greeting other dogs, playing with his own family human or dog; in fact he will not be interested in anything other than the next throw of the ball.

You frequently see owners looking rather smug as their dog walks glued to their side, with eyes like golf balls fixed on the ball lobber clutched in his human's hand. You know the owner is thinking to himself, *Look at how well my dog walks to heel – haven't I trained him well?*

There are two points here. Firstly, the dog is not enjoying himself as he should – he is extremely stressed, with nothing in his head other than the obsessive need to chase the ball. Secondly, if anyone were to take the ball lobber from his owner and walk away with it, the dog – far from being connected to his human – would follow without even caring that the person on the end of the ball lobber has changed.

It's fine to play gentle fetch (with puppies of course, you would roll the ball a short distance to avoid over-stressing growing bones and joints), but better still, play Find It, as this uses all the natural abilities of scent tracking and team work in a rather more gentle manner – and it avoids any potential ball obsession. All dogs have noses, the longer the nose the more scent receptors they have. Very short-nosed dogs are at a disadvantage: they cannot invariably carry a ball as they breathe through their mouths and their sense of smell is compromised, so use a toy appropriate to their physical abilities.

Paws for Thought

Obsessions and fear can take many forms, but there is always a reason why – and almost always they come about as a result of something we have introduced to the puppy. In the case of almost everything except fear-based obsessions, it will generally be something which started off as a bit of fun, but quickly turned sour. Obsessions are stressful and exhausting for all concerned, and it is our responsibility to do what it takes to undo the harm which (very often) we have caused.

Chasing animals, dogs and toys

Dogs have a huge prey drive, they chase things that move. To prevent them chasing the wrong thing, you first need to teach recall so your puppy will come when called (instructions for this on pages 83–5 and 105–6). The other important thing is that if you always teach your puppy to chase a ball to bring back to you, you're teaching him to respond to movement. You are also playing a mindless game that never changes and never challenges his brain.

The game of Don't Chase It in Chapter 13 (pages 87–8) is designed to help with this. As he becomes accomplished at it, neither a still ball nor a moving ball will flick his 'chase' drive – it's all about you.

Chasing lights

Chasing lights on the wall and barking usually has its roots in puppyhood. The way to prevent it is simply to not flick a light around a room. It only gets your puppy obsessed and stressed. In recent months, a laser torch for dogs has come on the market. It is neither funny to play with this nor good for your dog's head.

A puppy looks very cute when (usually quite by chance so far as the human is concerned) it catches sight of a spot of light thrown by a wristwatch. As the human moves his hand, so the light moves across the wall. The puppy follows the light, nose glued to the wall, often licking or trying to catch it in its teeth.

The unthinking human often zones in to what his puppy is doing and finds it hilarious – and laughs, moves the light around deliberately and encourages the puppy to continue, which of course raises the level of his excitement.

After a few months, the hilarity has turned to frustration – and panic when the sun appears! You often find a light-obsessed dog sitting facing the wall just waiting with bated breath for the light to appear – often for hours. More often than not he has expanded his range to chasing the shadows thrown by the sun, because by this time the desperate owner has taken to always wearing long sleeves – a sad state of affairs.

To cure this takes time and patience. Each time the dog focuses on the light, call him to you. If this does not happen, then gently go to him from the side, so as not to alarm him, and encourage him to follow you to another room. Then redirect him to a calmer game. You need to divert his attention to something more interesting than his mindless obsession.

You will have to persevere, but with time any obsession can be broken. Your dog will be so much happier for the break. But better yet, don't allow the obsession to start.

Stress or fear-based obsessions – compulsive licking, tail chasing, etc.

Sometimes an obsession can become rooted, not as a result of 'play gone wrong' but for more fundamental reasons. Obsessions born out of a puppy seeking 'coping' mechanisms, because the world has become so confusing or frightening, are the saddest of all. They can take many, and sometimes bizarre, forms.

It might be compulsive licking of a paw or chasing his tail. It could be taking an old piece of cloth into his mouth, cradling it with his paws and zoning out into a place in his head where the bewildering world cannot touch it. Or it could be any one of a hundred activities. The root cause is that the dog has found a way to partially relieve the intolerable stress of the moment.

These behaviours grow and become obsessions.

Prevention as ever is better than cure. As you introduce your puppy to your world, always take note of his body language and see if he is being pushed too far. If he is displaying any bizarre behaviours, stop, redirect your puppy away and hold still for calm, until his focus returns to you. Do not laugh at these behaviours; they are an indication of stress.

The only way to 'cure' obsession of any kind is to remove the cause of the stress: to gently take the fear and confusion away, and show your dog that he can relax and put his trust in you.

If he chews or licks his paw (or any other part of his anatomy), or in any way 'self-harms', then he has chosen this method to relieve his stress and self-soothe. Use this. He feels the need to chew, so give him something which will satisfy this need without harming himself – a bone or deer antler are perfect.

If the redirection works on its own, leave him be. If it doesn't, make the chew more interesting by moving it around, making it a game. When he engages fully on his chewing, leave him to get on with it.

If he is pacing or chasing his tail, then simply take him by the collar to stop the spin and then gently hold his side. This lets him feel your calm and follow suit. You're there for him when he is in a pickle.

You will probably notice that tail chasing or paw chewing, etc., arises when something has changed. Maybe someone just entered or left the room?

Take time to see what stresses your dog out. Be aware when he is using coping strategies for what he sees as stressful situations, even if *you* do not see them as stressful!

Maybe he'd love a den under a table, or a covered crate – that might be all he needs. A place that is just his, and of course someone who understands.

If your child was stressed, if they were manically biting their nails or pulling out their hair, looking terrified and panic running, would you sit back and laugh? Or would you take time to watch and understand? You'd hold them and be there for them until they're calm.

Obsessive barking at cars

Barking madly at cars, lorries and motor bikes, is almost always caused by too much, and too prolonged, exposure to these things when the puppy is not ready. Follow all the step-by-step instructions to introduce your puppy to the (really very frightening) noises of the street in Chapter 15. Make sure you take things slowly.

Paws for Thought

Remember your puppy is at street level and does not see things the way you do!

House Training

By following the instructions in Chapter 8, pages 53–4, your puppy will usually be housetrained by four months of age. He should have great bladder control by then, although you may get the odd accident if you're not vigilant. If by four months you are still experiencing accidents, ask your vet to check if there is a bladder infection – especially for females. If this is negative, then you have a behavioural issue – most probably from not being diligent enough in showing what's expected of him. Go back to Chapter 8 and follow the instructions closely.

Why Doesn't He Come When I Call?

If recall isn't working, it is likely that something like this has happened:

When you first brought your puppy home, just about everything he did seemed terribly cute. How could you resist him? Every time he came to you, you stroked and made a fuss of him. You hardly ever called him into your space. Just about the only thing you disliked was when he chewed something. You ploughed in and told him off, or called him to come, but he was so busily engrossed in his chosen activity that he just didn't hear you. He probably wouldn't have understood what you wanted anyway. Out in the garden there were more exciting smells and things to be discovered – he recalled sometimes but not always, as there were some wonderfully smelly mole hills. You then

started to take him out and about on his lead, and he pulled to investigate everything. You then let him off the lead to have a run around
in the park. He'd sniff and sniff, and you would call – and sometimes
he came and sometimes he didn't.

What he has learned is that he can either respond to his name or not.
If you allow him to think that this is the way to go on, his recall will
become progressively worse until, by the time he reaches six months
of age, he will stick both paws up at you every time you request his
presence and carry on with whatever he's doing.

We also often see owners calling their dogs only to turn away and
offer no praise when their little friend returns!

If you find that your puppy's recall is becoming selective, go back
to recall training in Chapter 12 (pages 83–5) and Chapter 15 (pages
105–6). Keep it fun, and be patient and consistent.

Paws for Thought

If every time your puppy comes to you uninvited he gets a
cuddle, he will not learn to come when called. So if he is
approaching you, call him, so it turns into you inviting him
to join you.

If you don't practise recall in the home environment you
are very unlikely to get it when out and about. Your
puppy will learn to blank you when you really need
him with you as he matures.

Reactive When on Lead

There are two scenarios here. If your puppy is simply pulling, bound-
ing and yapping, he's got no self-control (understandably at his age)
and is frustrated that he can't do what he wants when he wants. This

is where the game of Follow Me is needed in more low-stimulus environments, where you have a better chance of him listening to you. With this game he will learn that following his human is a fun thing to do.

In the second scenario, many dogs and puppies are non-confrontational when walking off lead, but aggressive when on. In dogs we call it aggressive, but in humans we call it angry or insecure – be understanding; he's not naughty just out of his comfort zone and feeling vulnerable. This is because when they feel uncertain about a situation, they don't trust the animal (you) on the other end of the lead to make the right decision. When shackled by a piece of rope and unable to act on their own instincts, it is of paramount importance to have implicit trust in the human on the other end of the rope. Your actions need to mirror the ones they would take if they were free to do so, so that you are perceived as a good decision maker in their eyes.

When you come across an uncertain situation, take exactly the same course of safe action each time: curve away, avoiding the 'threat', simultaneously inviting in a cheery voice for him to follow you, and then gently and quietly praise him for coming with you – if he does so calmly.

If he is stressed, and still focusing on the threat, walk on and move off in a different direction. When at a safe distance from the 'danger', spend a little time in silent Follow Me. Ensure you are looking down towards him – then, when he looks to you and sees your happy face, the connection is regained with ease. Your dog will correctly interpret your calm unflustered action as meaning that the 'threat' is actually nothing to become worried about.

Reward with food if you like when you have his focus. Bribing to achieve focus is only a quick fix, as any bond being created will be between your puppy and the treat in your pocket. He may focus for a split second for the food reward, but the tastiest treat will not trump the whiff of real danger – and that is when your puppy needs to call on the learned and uncluttered response of putting his trust in a confident and secure leader.

Separation Anxiety

Separation anxiety is very common, taking on many different guises. They include:

- Constant pacing about.
- The odd whine and then flopping down, to repeat the exercise again five minutes later.
- Scratching at the door.
- Going from whining to barking and howling.
- Becoming destructive.
- Peeing and pooping when alone in the house.

Destructive behaviour is the most heartbreaking manifestation. It not only takes the form of ripping up the house, but dogs can actually find windows to escape from causing themselves physical injury.

Mental distress of this kind is very common indeed and we need to ensure that your puppy grows up to be happy in his own skin, with or without you. Puppies enjoy companionship, and there are a proportion of these dogs who just need a doggy friend – but in many cases this is not the solution. They want *you* and feel lost without you.

It is important not to let your puppy follow you everywhere from day one. You have to show them you are not needy, and in doing so they'll know that they don't need to fret when, at times, they are without your companionship.

Even if he is asleep in his bed, shut doors behind you when you leave a room – even if you're only popping to the toilet. (When we say shut doors this is only for short periods of time, as your puppy needs you, and needs to feel part of the family, not banished constantly. He also needs to be with you to learn that not everything involves him.)

Watch your puppy's body language, and learn to recognise the difference between the actions of a puppy who *wants* to be with you, and one who *needs* to be with you.

In the first case, you may wander over to the computer (for example) and within a short time you will suddenly find that your pup has at some point quietly moved to join you. This is fine – he just feels that the nicest place to be is at your side, but it is a relaxed choice, not a desperate need.

The puppy who has a compulsive need to be with you will have had one eye and ear cocked at all times, ready and waiting for your move. When it comes he will immediately leap to his feet and follow you. This poor puppy is never truly relaxed. Do this future dog a kindness and take the preventative actions necessary to stop this need arising. If it is already there, work to relieve him of this responsibility.

One Paw at a Time: Preventing Separation Anxiety

◆ If you are sitting in a room with your puppy, do not be completely static. Make a point of moving around a bit, standing up and moving to another seat. Do not look at the puppy when you do this as this will be inviting him to join you. The aim is to be able to walk round a room freely without your puppy reacting – your puppy needs to be relaxed when things that do not involve him are occurring.

◆ Do not look at your puppy when you get up from your chair to go anywhere in the house. By all means put your hand up to him as you leave; this helps enormously by reducing the stress of a leave.

◆ When you leave a room, shut the door to show your puppy you do not need him with you.

◆ If you are going to be in the next room for any longer than it takes to go to the bathroom, then go back and simply open the door, showing your puppy he can join you if he wishes. He will most probably join you.

◆ Do not immediately look at him, just let him potter. Then you can call him over for a massage, when you are ready and he is minding his own business.

The only sure way to really know how settled your dog is when you are out is to video them. 'Taking the sting out of leaving', in Caroline's first book, *Why Does My Dog Do That?*, is a method used to cure separation anxiety. But it's much better to prevent it from the off, if you can.

Overtired and Overstimulated Puppies

Your puppy needs quiet time throughout the day to sleep, but you may need to teach him to switch off.

Come the evening, if you have an overstimulated puppy, you may find he flicks from one reaction to the next – bugging, poking, racing all over you. If you are feeding him appropriately, then this behaviour is down to overtiredness.

Keep his day fun but calm. If he becomes over the top, or you've revved him up, do not buy into this behaviour. Instead follow the instructions for Mouthing, Nibbling and Biting in Chapter 11 (pages 80–1).

Fear of Adults and Children

Puppies are not born with aggressive reactions. We create these by putting them in uncomfortable situations and failing to recognise their distress. Never force prolonged eye contact on a puppy, and never make it endure unwanted close physical contact, especially with a stranger. Everyone should treat your puppy with respect, and learning should be guided and not forced with anger.

Dogs don't meet each other eye to eye. They only make prolonged eye contact when they have something which they want to convey to the recipient. This could be 'play with me' – which will always be accompanied by playful body language – or 'I want you to do this or that, or to come with me', again accompanied by the appropriate body language (think of the famous, and much derided, line from every Lassie movie ever written: 'I think he wants us to follow him!').

However, for dogs, prolonged eye contact with a stiff, 'tall' and still body stance is almost always a prelude to confrontation, so prolonged eye contact from a human without the explanatory body language is confusing to your puppy, and can be interpreted as aggressive. It will make him very uncomfortable. Forcing eye contact and very close contact with strangers can very readily result in fear aggression as they move through adolescence into adulthood.

A human who visits may be utterly unaware of how threatening their behaviour is seen as. For instance, a guest may stare down at the puppy and reach out their hands, perhaps saying, 'Oh don't worry, it's only me.' This will cause the puppy to back off and drop eye contact by facing away to try and appease the human, but the guest keeps moving closer. At this point the puppy will invariably urinate through fear.

The puppy is frightened. If the guest doesn't take the hint, the puppy barks and barks some more, but the human may often repeat the very action that makes the puppy more fearful. This is how we make a puppy into a nervous barking adolescent and adult who will, potentially, bite.

Think of a child. If he was avoiding eye contact, backing away from a visitor and even screaming the house down, would you approach him? You might crouch down, so you are not such a big giant, and call him to you in a gentle manner. Or simply stop staring and concentrate on talking to the mother. The child would settle down, reassured that you are not about to get too close for comfort. If you were the mother, you would most likely probably pick up your child and hold him close – but you wouldn't then encourage your guest to loom over and touch him.

Similarly, as the owner of a puppy, you need to stand between the focus of fear and your dog, to show you are protection. When you invite someone into your home, you need to keep a very close eye on your puppy's communication signals. Never thrust your puppy into accepting the attentions of humans, however well-intentioned your guest might be. When raised with the philosophy of 'get used to it', these nervous dogs grow up to bite.

Fear of Noise

Of course your puppy will flinch when he hears a loud clatter, but don't make a mountain out of a molehill. Be unflustered – it will show him there is nothing to worry about. See Chapter 11 on acclimatising in the home.

Whether it is thunder or fireworks or a backfiring car, make nothing of it. If you're at home and your puppy runs to you, all you have to do is be there with him. Hold him gently and make no verbal fuss. If you stroke him to try and comfort him, he is more likely going to take that as praise for the fear rather than comfort. Sit next to your pup and, with hands on sides, massage deep if you like, but don't try to pacify with a soft voice. You need to sound and be assertive.

Out and about, again, sound assertive with a 'Come on this way', and turn and walk away from the sound.

Fear of Dogs

If during socialising with other puppies and dogs we choose the wrong playmate, we can end up in trouble. Nine times out of ten, puppies become dog aggressive because they had an aggressive encounter with another dog. Choose your pup's friends wisely – the same age, same size. If there is a bully in the mix, don't make a big deal about it. Simply removing the bully for a short hold until he's calm, then releasing him to play again is teaching manners with other dogs.

Puppies can play rough, learning how hard to bite and what they can get away with. Don't fly in there with the first yelp that is them communicating to each other. If your pup has had enough, he will more than likely run to you – at this point, hold the chaser for a moment of calm. Pups can play for a very long time, as the adrenaline rises. You need to be there to show them that time is up – and not just for behavioural reasons: tired limbs and ligaments can damage easily.

Paws for Thought

If we had a bad experience with something as a child, we grow up scared of it. If your parents were fearful of anything, they would teach you to be afraid of that too. You trust their actions and their fear. If no one helped you through your fears, you'd have to find your own solutions – either to fight or run away. If you had no other option, you'd fight.

Your puppy will behave in same way as you would have as a child. If you are calm, and lead them away from situations they find scary, they will learn to be calm and to trust you.

Out and about, don't encourage your puppy to go and play and meet every dog you see – you don't know what the other dogs are like, and you'll set yours up to fail. Think about it this way: would you tell your child to go greet and play with every child he sees when you go out? Of course not. So find friends who you know have lovely dogs, and then your pup can play and grow up with them on walks. Failing this, speak to your vet nurse who may be able to suggest someone.

Your puppy needs you and only you and your family. Be his playmate, his friend and protector.

Attention-Seeking Behaviours

Attention-seeking behaviours can become apparent when dynamics change. For instance, when visitors arrive and you have your attention on them instead of your puppy. If your puppy (or child for that matter) succeeds in getting your attention off the visitor and onto them, you have made them the most important being at that time. Think about when you've had a conversation with a parent, and their child comes up and butts in. If the parent takes their attention straight off you, without an apology, it feels rude and unthinking.

Like children, we need our puppies to grow up knowing they will get everything they want and need, but in our time.

As we have said earlier, do not pander to a demanding puppy when he asks to play or asks for a cuddle – disregard his attention-seeking behaviour and, when he gives you space, recall him quickly afterwards, so it is *you* who has decided it's time for whatever. This also helps him learn recall. It is also very important to get your visitors to direct their attention to you, and not your puppy.

We need to teach our puppy that all good things come to those who are patient. When you are rushed, things go wrong or you are forgetful. So slow things down. Don't jump to attention and go 'Yes, Sir!' every time your puppy wants; he will only grow more demanding – something that will be all the more difficult to handle when he is fully grown.

Barking, Growling, Grumbling

Puppies learn to bark. They bark for many reasons, and it is up to you to decide what is acceptable barking and what is not.

We accept barking as something 'that puppies do', in the same way as we know children squeal and scream when they become over-excited. However, humans are naturally much more vocal than dogs – we communicate largely through speech, whereas dogs predominantly use body language. And, even so, when our children become so over-stimulated that they resort to screaming and squealing we very quickly say, 'OK, now calm down a little – you are becoming overexcited' – and we gently bring them back down to earth. We know that there comes a point when the stress of even an enjoyable pursuit becomes unaccept-able and potentially harmful to a child, either physically or emotionally.

Puppies are no different – in fact, because dogs are naturally far less vocal than humans, if your puppy is barking (aka, yipping in a high-pitched 'puppy' way) excessively, it is time to investigate the reasons and do something about it.

Both of us have observed litters that we have bred, and we have seen that puppy barking is never random – even if it appears to be, there is always a reason.

If a puppy is trying to encourage a sleepy or uninterested littermate to play, he will do so firstly by using 'play with me' body language – play bows, gambolling around the 'target', etc. It is usually further down the line that any barking occurs, either because the littermate doesn't want to play, so the puppy gets frustrated and ups the ante, or if play is in full swing and something occurs that causes an excess of stimulation. This could be that the 'playee' has taken possession of a valued trophy, and won't let the other have it, or that the other puppy has had enough and wants to rest. Or that one puppy has inadver-tently been hurt and therefore knocks the game on the head, and the other is just not ready to stop, or one of a dozen other reasons.

The point is that, in this situation, anything more than the occa-sional few yips is a result of overstimulation or frustration, and will be regulated by the puppies themselves – one simply refuses to continue the game, and the other will gradually wind down – or the mother will step in to call a halt.

A litter of puppies will often give a united chorus of barking when they encounter an alien object. This could be anything from a hedge-hog to a broom, and it almost always occurs when the mother is not around for the puppies to look to for guidance. Make no mistake, cute though it looks, the puppies are in deadly earnest – they are attempting to protect themselves by a show of strength and their adrenaline levels are sky high. When the mother hears the commotion, she will always appear and, if the 'danger' is no danger at all, either let the puppies work things out for themselves or step in if the puppies start 'in fighting' as a result of the fear-induced excitement caused by the threat.

There are many more scenarios which may cause an adult dog to bark, but in a puppy, at this early stage, you can be pretty safe in assuming that the root cause will be either fear, frustration, boredom, loneliness or overstimulation.

In a natural setting, the mother stays with her pups for many months and continues (along with the rest of the pack) to educate her offspring in an instinctive, progressive way. Every new occurrence serves as a learning experience. The puppy is secure and safe in looking to its mother, siblings and other pack members for guidance, and excessive frustrated/fearful/attention-seeking barking does not occur.

Without a mother or other canines to guide him, your puppy looks to you. If your puppy is barking excessively, then look for the underlying reason, and take the stress which is causing the problem away.

Possible causes for excessive barking:

Barking from overstimulation and excitement

If you play for too long, or in a way that winds your puppy up to the point where he is frantically yapping and charging around, do not think that this is 'fun' – it is a puppy vastly overstimulated, out of control and stressed.

If a child reaches the state during play where he has become overstimulated and is doing himself and his playmates no favours, you would call him away initially, and if he was too 'in the zone' to respond you would go to him and gently remove him from the situation.

Do likewise with your puppy.

At first, gentle restraint will probably be necessary as all he wants is to get back to the game, and he will be straining his neck to see what is going on and ignoring you completely. But, gradually, your calm presence and soothing sensible words will percolate through, and he will start to connect. At this stage you can gradually bring him down to a safe level, and either distract him by introducing a less stressful game to play or let him back to his playmates in a less manic frame of mind.

What you would *not* do is to yell at him to 'Calm down!' or shout 'Get here!', or grab him and drag him away with your recriminations ringing in his ears. Doing this would be fuelling his hysteria, winding him up to the point of tears and tantrums, and completely spoiling what could have gone back to being an enjoyable and rewarding lesson in playing with his peers without conflict.

The next time he plays, your child will remember how you behaved. If you chose the first course of action, he will realise that it is better and more enjoyable to not become manic.

If you did take the second option, he may try to get in as much 'play' as he can before the inevitable shouted recriminations and dragging away occur. Other children will almost certainly react to his 'over the top' antics by trying to avoid him, and this will make him redouble his efforts to make them play with him and pave the path to his becoming a frustrated and unhappy child who desperately wants, but does not know how, to fit in.

If your puppy becomes hysterical and barks madly when playing (either with canine chums or human), firstly call him to you. If this does not work, go to him and quietly remove him. Turn him away to you in order to break his focus. Then, when he starts to calm down and reconnect to you, either engage him in a less lively game – Follow Me is good here, it re-establishes calm and connection, and engages his mind – or calmly lead him away and massage.

When he is calm and responsive again, you can praise him quietly and perhaps take him back to his chums for a less manic session. If he returns to the barking and overexcitement, simply repeat – but this time without returning to the scene of the 'crime'.

You must remain calm and controlled. Lack of control from you will feed his hysteria and establish an unacceptable pattern.

You deal with the barking by addressing the whole situation – do this and, as acceptable 'rules of engagement' begin to be established, the barking will take care of itself.

Attention-seeking barking

A puppy who constantly yaps for attention has either learned to do this because it gets results – play or attention on demand – or because he is so desperate for you to take notice of him that it is his last resort. You are actually lucky if this last one is the case, because many puppies who receive inappropriate or zero interaction will just shut down and go into their shell.

Give your puppy appropriate attention, education and controlled, constructive playtime and free time. Show him how to fit into your family without stress and you will not have an endlessly yapping puppy.

It is interesting to note that with all the puppies from the litters we have bred – puppies who stay with their mother for a lifetime – we have never encountered any kind of excessive yapping. In fact, in one notable case, Lesley nearly jumped out of her skin the first time Kia (a 'puppy' of two years) barked at the sound of the doorbell. Her mother was the most laid-back, well-balanced dog in the world, and always gave a warning of intruders but then allowed the humans to deal with it, so Kia had a perfect role model. She had never been influenced by a stressed older dog, so grew up slowly and comprehensively. She enjoyed her puppyhood and adolescence and was content to leave the door 'to the grown-ups' until she reached maturity herself.

Of course very few puppies have this kind of seamless graduation from puppy to adult, with a mother who can educate them in a completely natural and stress-free way, but we can do the best we can for them by acting as a surrogate — learning what makes them tick, and recognising the difference between fun and stress in our puppies.

Loneliness and boredom

In a natural environment a puppy would never be alone (nor in most cases would an adult dog). Unfortunately it is rarely possible in our human world to be with our dogs constantly, so gradually, and with empathy, you will need to accustom your puppy to very short periods of your absence. Do not leave your puppy for anything more than about 15 minutes to start with, and slowly building up to a maximum of three hours during the day as he matures. Start this only when he is secure in his new home – this is why we advise your taking a period of leave when you first take your puppy to live with you. See pages 128–9 on preventing separation anxiety.

Make time to educate your puppy – not only is this essential as he needs to learn to live in the human world, it also stimulates his mind, avoiding boredom. This is best achieved in the early months through age-appropriate play, as described in Chapter 12. Learning through play is considered the basis for more structured education for both children and puppies. A bored, lonely and therefore understimulated puppy may resort to endless barking to while away the hours.

Frustration barking

Do not put your puppy in situations which cause him frustration. From the outset, show him the way you wish him to behave and work as closely with his natural instincts as possible. Frustration often is a result of not knowing what is required, trying 'to get it right', but constantly failing and being reprimanded for it.

If you have children, do not allow them to tease the puppy. They may think it hilarious to constantly thwart and challenge the little soul because the ensuing frantic behaviour appears so cute and funny. It isn't, and this and overstimulation though play with unsupervised children is a major cause of stress or fear (and the accompanied barking) in puppies.

Fear barking

Puppies naturally look to their mother or an older pack member when they encounter a new situation, object or any previously unknown scenario. They take from the reaction of their elders the correct way to deal with this. You are the surrogate parent, so make sure that your reaction to their uncertainty reflects the reaction you want from them.

Never deluge them with too many sights, sounds or situations. As we explained in Chapter 15, take their introduction to the alien human world slowly and, when they show fear, calmly show them that you see nothing to be afraid of. If there is cause for alarm, deal with the situation in a quietly authoritative way. In other words, show them that they need not address anything that causes them fear; they only need to look to you and follow your lead.

When they mature, if you have brought them up correctly, they will be well equipped to deal with everyday occurrences on their own – only looking to you when they are uncertain of how to act. This unconditional trust that you will protect and guide them should become second nature.

The world can be a scary place to a young puppy – particularly the strange and noisy creatures and machines which inhabit the human world, and also strange adult dogs (and any other creatures, for that matter) can be a source of worry to a puppy. He is still living much more closely with his natural instincts than later, when age and acclimatisation begin to demystify the world. These instincts tell him that his adult pack members will take all the responsibility for avoiding anything that can be a threat. In the natural world, these same canine pack members would gradually educate him to the workings of his domain – and that means very restricted access to the wider world until he is very much older than the age at which *we* expose puppies to scary new sights and sounds.

When confronted with anything which he perceives to be a threat, your puppy's natural reaction will be to slide away and let the adults take care of the danger or, if he has no adult to shield him, to try to drive it away by a show of strength – barking and a threatening body stance.

For more on outside fears, return to Chapter 15, pages 101–4. For inside fears, Chapter 11, pages 68–9 will help. For fearing adults coming into your home, also see Chapter 11, pages 72–3.

Paws for Thought

Unnecessary Gadgets to Correct Behaviour

Although (thank goodness) electric shock collars, prong collars, citronella collars, air horns, rattle tubes and other instruments of torture have pretty much fallen from grace, it is amazing how many people still favour the good old 'squirt in the face' with a water pistol, air pump or similar as a method of curtailing barking. They pat themselves on the back for not using noxious substances such as citronella, as 'only water' can do no harm . . . can it?

The idea is that these 'tools' stop the dog in his tracks and stops the barking. And of course they *do* (at first, until the dog gets used to it) for a second or two – which is often enough time to get past the reason for the barking. But the barking recommences at the next trigger.

Of course a squirt in the face, or similar, will cause the dog to think, 'What the **** was that??!!' and stop for a moment. It is a distraction, nothing more.

The dog has learned nothing, except that every so often he will get a squirt in the face for no reason. It is a moot point as to whether he even connects the squirt with the barking, and certainly it does nothing to further the bond between human and dog – quite the opposite.

The level of tension almost certainly will rise, causing even more frantic barking at the next 'threat'. As the dog is usually on lead at the time, he has no access to his instinctive reactions of 'freeze or flight', which is stressful in itself. He may also connect the shock of the squirt with the object or creature of its focus at the time of the squirt, thus creating a fear or aggression toward that object.

Imagine the outcry if we used a water pistol to control our children's behaviour. If you're still not convinced, try this: If your partner is in 'verbal diarrhoea' mode, boring you witless about his or her football team/new shoes/latest office gossip, instead of diplomatically steering the conversation somewhere more interesting, try squirting them in the face with a washing-up bottle full of water. Then say, 'It's OK – it's only water! Now, let's talk about something else.'

Good luck with that one!

Mouthing and Biting – Dog to Dog and Dog to Human

We first looked at how to teach your dog not to mouth and bite in Chapter 11 (pages 80–1). If your dog hasn't learned bite inhibition by about sixteen weeks of age, they will be on the way to holding too hard, which constitutes a bite whether meant in malice or not.

Bite inhibition is first learned when in the litter, primarily where it concerns other canines. However, with humans a puppy must learn that no 'teeth on skin' is acceptable, and we do this in the early days by yelping, turning away and immediately withdrawing ourselves. Later on, if the lesson has not been thoroughly implemented and the puppy (now no longer a puppy, really) is still nipping, a yelp will only serve to wind him up further – you sound like prey. So simply refuse to interact further. Remove yourself by leaving the room or just walking away. A period of completely disregarding (with disapproving body language; stiff, upright and facing away) any attempt to re-engage with you should follow, and this should slowly teach him that nipping does not get him anywhere.

If you react angrily, or with retaliation, you are buying into his mindset, and this is not useful at all.

One Paw at a Time: Biting after Sixteen Weeks

◆ Ensure you are not revving your dog up to behave like this.
◆ Be calm and respond with no eye contact or verbal reprimand. Just walk away from his space.
◆ If he continues, walk out of the room and shut the door you both need time to take a breath.
◆ Come back in after five seconds of quiet, but do not engage with him until any jumping or demanding attention is over and you can call him to you. You really need professional one-to-one help if it has got to this stage.

Head Shy Issues

If you constantly lunge for his collar to correct him you will make your puppy head shy, and this can lead to mouthing and biting. The collar is only there to attach the ID tag and, occasionally, to gently redirect. Do not use it to drag your puppy to where you want him.

Instead, it is always better to call your puppy to you and praise him when he comes. Do not lunge forward with your arms to grab him, but encourage him to come right to you before you give a reward of praise. Not only are you stopping any unacceptable behaviour, but you are enabling your puppy to do something that is worthy of praise.

Car or Motion Sickness

Car sickness is most prevalent in puppies rather than adult dogs, and research suggests this is because the balance mechanisms in the inner ear are not fully developed. Many will outgrow it by twelve months of age. But it is also said that car sickness is more to do with stress than with motion.

It is hard to avoid car journeys or public transport for vet trips, or when going to the park or on holiday, so it is a great idea to introduce him to short stress-free journeys early on. Ideally, he will have been on short journeys with his littermates and mother, but if this has not occurred just take things slowly, and don't make it a big deal.

One Paw at a Time: Getting Car Journeys Right

- Before you begin, choose a time when your puppy is calm with – vitally – an empty stomach!
- You will need two humans for a car journey – one to drive and one to be with your puppy.
- Have a window slightly open for constant fresh air, and ensure the car is not hot and the vents are not blowing.
- Don't soothe your puppy verbally, just hold him gently yet firmly.
- Play soft classical music that has been played previously during stress-free times.
- You may like to give your puppy a herbal remedy if he salivates a lot.

Jumping Up

Puppies jump up at people because (a) they are trying to get your eye contact, (b) they have not been shown it is impolite, and (c) because this is what they do to their returning mother and other pack members. As humans we do not appreciate this natural behaviour. Just as with children, who will raggle your arm, look up at you and push in to get attention, dogs do this until they have been shown that patience gets rewarded – and this takes time.

We need to educate our puppies not to jump up because there are many people who are very frightened of dogs. Others just don't like them, or don't want their clothes covered in mud. If a human reacts badly to this, it is not their fault or your puppy's – it is yours.

If you raise your voice in a stern 'Get down!' you are punishing your puppy. This may result in him jumping up even quicker next time, before you have a chance to react. Anxiety rises, and jumping up becomes a habit of anxiety, as your puppy doesn't quite know what to do.

Instead, from an early stage and without a fuss, put your puppy's paws back on the ground. Practise with people you know, and instruct them to keep talking to you, ignoring your puppy, until he is calm. Then they can call him over for a greeting. With bigger puppies it is best to walk into their space – and remember no eye contact. Do not turn your back and walk away; they have taken your space . . . that's rude!

One Paw at a Time: Jumping Up at Sixteen Weeks Plus

You will now need to be a little firmer with your body language. Don't turn your back and walk away. It works sometimes but not all the time, and you have just shown your puppy he can push you about. Instead:

◆ Move a pace towards your dog with no eye contact or speech.
◆ Turn side on and move forwards (crab-like) to take his space. He will remove himself out of your way.
◆ Call him to you for a gentle fuss, so he can see he gets your attention for coming to you when asked, but not for jumping up at you.
◆ You can also use this technique if he jumps up towards the kitchen units. Again, use your body to brush him sideways off the units, walk him away using your body, until he is at a respectful distance, then continue as above.

◆ Many dogs are a pest when you are cooking; this procedure shows your puppy from the start that he stands away from food preparation.

As your dog sees he gets nothing out of jumping up, he will eventually decide that it is not worth even trying.

Mugging Guests

Many advise a visitor to try to make a puppy feel better about their entrance by giving them a food treat. This can teach your puppy to mug everyone who comes into your home. If you encourage people out and about to give him treats too it can result in even more mugging behaviour – your dog thinks everyone is a vending machine.

We've seen many dogs who have no self-control. They have learned to be bullies, muggers and thieves of possessions and space, and this all comes from having the wrong teachers.

We want our dogs, like our children, to earn what they have and respect others for what they have – everything and anything isn't yours just for the asking. Review Chapter 11, pages 72–3 for instructions for visiting guests.

Paws for Thought

Treats

Treats must be used as an intermittent reward by the owner. Your dog must receive it for a job well done, not just because he is loved. Just as with us humans, if he works for what he gets, he won't take it for granted. The platinum rule when giving treats: reward, never bribe!

Frustration with Collar, Harness and Lead

For a puppy, wearing something round the neck is strange, and it is a pretty safe bet that he'll want to scratch it off. Many puppies will also want to bite their new lead.

If the breeder has marked the pups by collar colour then your job has been done already. They have got used to a collar while diverted from the sensation by playing with their siblings. But you will still need to introduce your puppy to the harness after a week or two. However, collar, harness and lead introductions should be pretty straightforward if you make great associations with their presence. In Chapter 11 we went through the steps of introducing your puppy to the collar, harness and then lead. If he's feeling frustrated with any of this 'kit', take him back a few steps, and rebuild gradually.

Possessiveness of Furniture or Space

It's your choice whether to allow your puppy on the sofa or bed, and the way you deal with each teaches him to respect your decisions.

If you do not want your puppy on the furniture, ever, remove him without speech or eye contact. By doing this it doesn't turn into a game. (Do not let your puppy either jump up or down from furniture, as it is not good for his growing body.) Now he's on the floor, gently guide him towards his bed or a blanket next to you on the floor, showing him that this is where you'd like him to rest. Hold him there while he relaxes, and then simply remove your hand.

If he is asleep, make sure he is aware of your presence before trying to remove him – you don't want to go take hold of him when he is in the land of nod and freak him out!

By removing him quietly without speech or eye contact, you will have shown him, very certainly in your puppy's mind, that the sofa is not a place for him. If you said 'Get down!' or 'No!' your puppy has you attention and therefore *his* action has worked.

Have a bed for him in every room where he is allowed, so he has a focal point to settle, ideally in a nook away from the thoroughfare. Next to or behind a sofa or under a table is perfect.

If, however, you do want your dog on the sofa with you, ensure you have invited him – call him over and pick him up. This shows him that it is your sofa, and there will be no thoughts of possession on the part of your growing puppy.

Paws for Thought

If your puppy sits with you on furniture, it should be because you have invited him to join you, not because he has allowed you to join him!

Possessiveness of Food

Never ever take food away from a dog after you have given it. You gave it to him, let him get on with it – you will not make him possessive or aggressive towards food if you follow this advice.

We hear many people say that they can take food away as and when, their dog is fine – we say, they are playing with fire! Or they say, 'When I take a bone from my dog he growls, but that's fine.' Actually, he's not fine – he is giving you a warning. The next step is for him to bite.

It is a great idea to put extra food into his bowl while your puppy is eating, so that your hand is seen as giving and kind.

If you have brought your puppy up to have no food aggression you should have no problem removing an item of food (for example, a 'filched' bar of chocolate) if the occasion calls for it. He will respect your right to take it. The decision maker in the pack has all food rights, and your dog will understand this. If, however, you have any worries at all concerning his reaction, do not consider doing this. Only a dog who respects your right to do this will allow you to take food from him. If you have an adolescent who has started being food possessive, then information to help correct this behaviour is in Caroline's book *Why Does My Dog Do That?* Never put your hand in a food-aggressive dog's bowl or near his food.

Possessiveness with Toys

This follows the same rule as with food. If you constantly take but don't give, you will wind your puppy up.

If your puppy has something in his mouth you'd rather he didn't have, or it is dangerous, call him to you and swap for something he can chew, like a stag antler or a different toy he is allowed. You may need to go to him – with no eye contact approach him side on and swap for the allowed item.

By doing this, you are not snatching something of high value or turning events into a game of chase. You are calm and unpanicked, so won't also upset your puppy or give him an opportunity to use it as an attention-seeking tool.

For similar reasons, avoid the game of tug of war, as it not only winds your puppy up but encourages possessive behaviour.

Don't make it a big deal and your puppy won't either.

Being Possessive of the Owner

You create a possessive puppy with your actions.

◆ You spend the whole time standing to attention and going, 'Yes sir, no sir, three bags full sir!' to all your puppy's attention seeking.
◆ You allow him to jump up and sit on or next to you wherever you are, as and when he pleases.
◆ You allow him to follow you continually and becomes your constant shadow.

◆ You hold him in your lap or, when standing up, in your arms, while you interact with others: in his mind, your space becomes his space; his fears are also your fears.

With such behaviours, there is a great possibility that your puppy will grow up to become protective of you and of the space you inhabit. The result may be that when someone sits next to you, or even goes to shake your hand, he will jump into possessive action – and you will be left feeling rather embarrassed and making one excuse after another.

To ensure you don't get into this downwards spiral, which could well end up in court (whether it happens in your home or out and about), make sure you live your life with your dog on your terms. Get the dynamics right from the start.

This is all dependent on the personality of your dog, of course, and on his past experiences. Be a wise owner and take measures before you slip down this slippery slope – see the advice on the other possessive behaviours above.

If you are already in this position you need to show your adolescent dog that this behaviour is not acceptable. It must always be the 'favoured' person who corrects his behaviour, especially aggression, by guiding the dog away immediately. The dog has a connection to this person, he has claimed this person, so it must be this person who shows him that the 'unfavoured' human is to be respected, and that the favoured will not tolerate disrespect. If the unfavoured human tries to correct behaviour, it could end in tears, as the dog neither respects him nor wants him around.

If your Puppy Prefers One Member of the Family

All humans in the household should be gentle and kind, and sing off the same song sheet – following all the guidelines in this book.

If your puppy is a rescue it may have received rough handling from one particular gender and this may result in him preferring one member of your family over another. Don't take this personally!

Don't pour love into your puppy, he needs time to adjust and for you to be patient. By taking a back seat, your puppy will – in time – want to migrate towards you. Sit at his level on the floor, side on, with no eye contact and no stretching out to touch him. Read or chat or watch telly, so you are concentrating on something else, not him. Being allowed the time and space to adjust and settle, is what will help your little friend to trust you, and want to be with you.

When he comes to investigate you, and sniff around you, place your hand on the floor. After he sniffs it, tickle him under his chin, but let him back away too, as that may well be enough, or too much, to begin with. In this instance, we do suggest that a food reward be in your hand for him to take – it reinforces you are a nice chap or chapess.

A preference for one human over the other doesn't mean the 'unchosen one' should think 'he just does not like me'. Keep making unthreatening overtures of connection. Try to understand that it is his past experiences that have caused the unwillingness to engage – nothing personal. Keep the lines of communication open – just do not push things to happen before the puppy is ready.

Food Fussiness

Some puppy owners will not believe this exists, but it does happen! And, yes, your puppy's food fussiness is something you cause yourself.

If your dog has suddenly gone off his food and it is out of character then please visit your vet for advice. But if your pup is showing signs of food fussiness, remember they will not starve themselves, so you can simply leave them to eat the dinner or go hungry.

However, you can avoid any fussiness by following these simple rules:

One Paw at a Time: Perfect Mealtimes

◆ If you are using dry food, make sure that the pack is fresh and not opened for longer than two weeks. After this time it goes rancid and, understandably, your pup will probably refuse it.

◆ Make sure the area is quiet so your puppy can enjoy his meal without distractions.

◆ Give him a wholesome natural diet suitable for canines – we recommend biologically appropriate raw food (BARF) (see Resources for more information).

◆ Do not ask your puppy to sit before meal times – that is just human control and will bring about an anxiety to perform and then not eat. Wait for your puppy to stand still with no jumping. Moving towards him will help this happen.

◆ Then place the bowl down, so he has to walk to his food and make an effort. We all have to put effort into whatever we do; patience and movement are the powerful, meaningful tools here.

◆ Turn and step away a few paces, but stay in the room. When he has finished – i.e. when he has walked away from the bowl, whether it is all gone or not – remove the bowl.

◆ We advocate eating a small morsel before you put your pup's food down. Dogs do this to each other, one may stand back till the other has started to eat (you can see this if you have a group of dogs in your home, the one they respect more eats first and goes through a door first).

Paws for Thought: Wolfing it Down

This phrase came from the way wolves eat – they almost inhale their food. The quicker it gets down, the more certain they are to eat as much as they can. Many dogs do the same, and provided they are fed a natural diet this causes no problems.

A canine digestive system is perfectly designed to take huge amounts of food quickly and all in one go, but because many owners use dried food full of indigestible (for a canine stomach) carbohydrates, this causes problems. To avoid this, you can get bowls that have raised knobs that slow the feeding down or spread the food out on the floor. Always put a small amount of water with the food, so it is damp and can be swallowed with ease. Better still, give your puppy a natural canine diet then there will be no issue.

Conclusion

We hope that this book has helped in giving you the confidence to bring up your puppy in a relaxed and natural way. Try to use our guidelines without becoming too embroiled in 'I should not do this', 'I must not do that'. Above all, parenting your puppy should be light-hearted and fun.

Use your common sense, your knowledge of human children, your knowledge of what makes *you* happy, sad, fearful and angry, and of how recognising boundaries and learning discipline created a feeling of order and security for you when you were a child. Then use this to help you understand what motivates your puppy.

We hope we have shown you the fundamental drives of your puppy. You now know how to observe and take note of your puppy's individual personality, so you can go with the flow as much as you can without losing the necessary control that comes from being your puppy's 'parent'.

You know how to teach him new things while having fun, but you can also remove him calmly and confidently from situations that make him stressed – you can help him to keep safe.

When you achieve this balance, you will not fall into the trap of overreaction and micromanagement. There will be no shouting unless it's a genuine emergency, and no endless requests for repetition of mindless tasks. No creature is comfortable with his every action being under the microscope and analysed; this makes what should be a happy and mutually enriching relationship into a stress-filled endurance test.

Dogs and humans *like* each other, they have a natural affinity, a unique bond. So embrace this and use your natural instincts to play a big part when teaching your puppy.

It really is not so hard to do.

A prayer:

> 'Dear Lord, help me to be the kind of person my dog thinks I am.'

> (Anon.)

Resources

Nutrition and feeding

Honeys Natural Feeding Handbook for Dogs by Jonathan Self (Mammoth, 2011)

Raw Dog Food
www.rawdogfood.com

Rodney Habib pet nutrition blogger
www.rodneyhabib.com

Food suppliers

UK
www.honeysrealdogfood.com

www.naturalinstinct.com

USA
www.reelrawdog.com

Canada
www.planetpaws.ca

We prefer a natural raw food for our dogs but freezer space and being on holiday sometimes means we cannot do this. In the UK, these are two companies that produce a dry food that have a very small cabohydrate content and source human grade ingredients:

www.angellpetco.com

www.edenpetfoods.com

The Raw Feeding Directory (https://rawfeedingdirectory.com/) is a directory of raw supportive vets, suppliers and other dog-related businesses. There's also a breeders section, although it's not a focus at the time of writing.

The British Association of Homeopathic Veterinary Surgeons (www.bahvs.com/)

American Holistic Veterinary Medical Association (www.ahvma.org/) if you're planning on selling across the pond.

Vaccination

The World Small Animal Veterinary Association's Vaccination Guidelines for New Puppy Owners
www.wsava.org/sites/default/files/New%20Puppy%20Owner%20Vaccination%20Guidelines%20May%202013_0.pdf

Other useful articles:
www.dogsnaturallymagazine.com/revaccination-and-dogs

www.greenacreskennel.com/pet-health/vaccination-interviews-with-dr-ron-schultz-%E2%80%93-may-2013.html

www.canine-health-concern.org.uk/Jordan%20AHVMA%20Journal%20Summary%20of%20Schultz%20Presentation.pdf

Health and well-being

Dog Breed Health
A very comprehensive and up-to-date site with all the vital tests each and every breed should have had: www.dogbreedhealth.com

Paul Manktelow's website
www.vitalpethealth.co.uk

Canine Health Concern
www.canine-health-concern.org.uk

The People's Dispensary for Sick Animals Pet Health Advice
www.pdsa.org.uk/pet-health-advice

Neutering

Laura J. Sanborn's article is well worth a read so you can make
informed choices as to when is best to castrate or spay. Visit
www.naiaonline.org then search for 'spay' and click on the result
to her PDF.

Dog behaviour

This is our own blog, which of course we recommend for more information on dog behaviour:
www.puredoglisteners.com/blog

We are also on Facebook and YouTube.

The Ultimate Happy At Heel Harness

Designed by Caroline for pups over five months old:
www.ancol.co.uk

For puppies under five months old, use a soft-bank attachment
harness that is well padded.

Calming music for dogs

By Lisa Spector, the standard icalm is perfect:
http://throughadogsear.com/icalmdog/package-details/

Dog car crates and beds
UK
www.transk9.com

Memory foam beds for comfort and health from www.woofbed.co.uk

Register your pet
OCPIN Pet ID Tags

Paw'tected dog ID tags for global usage affiliated to www.doglost.co.uk. Uniquely coded cat, dog and luggage tags. www.ocpin.com

Fight against puppy farms
UK
Pup Aid
www.pupaid.org

RSPCA Reporting Cruelty
www.rspca.org.uk/utilities/contactus/reportcruelty

USA
ASPCA Reporting Animal Cruelty
www.aspca.org/fight-cruelty/report-animal-cruelty

Dog law
UK
The Kennel Club
www.thekennelclub.org.uk

Control of Dogs, The Law and You
www.doglaw.co.uk

USA
ASPCA State Animal Cruelty Laws
www.aspca.org/fight-cruelty/advocacy-center/state-animal-cruelty-laws

Animal Legal Defense Fund Animal Protection Laws of the USA and Canada
http://aldf.org/resources/advocating-for-animals/animal-protection-laws-of-the-united-states-of-america-and-canada/

Further reading

www.apa.org/news/press/releases/2009/08/dogs-think.aspx – article about Stanley Coren, PhD address 'How Dogs Think', at the American Psychological Association, 2009

Why Does My Dog Do That? Understand and Improve Your Dog's Behaviour and Build a Friendship Based on Trust by Caroline Spencer (Robinson, 2013)

Aggression In Dogs: Practical Management, Prevention and Behavior Modification by Brenda Aloff (Dogwise, 2004)

Canine Body Language: A Photographic Guide by Brenda Aloff (Dogwise, 2009)

The Emotional Lives of Animals by Marc Bekoff (New World Library, 2007)

Animals Make Us Human: Creating the Best Life for Animals by Temple Grandin (Houghton Mifflin, 2010)

The Complete Dog Massage Manual by Julia Robertson (Hubble & Hattie, 2010)

Exercising Your Puppy: A Gentle and Natural Approach by Julia Robertson (Hubble & Hattie, 2011)

On Talking Terms with Dogs: Calming Signals by Turid Rugaas (Dogwise, 2009)

Honeys Natural Feeding Handbook for Dogs by Jonathan Self (Mammoth, 2011)

Index